MW01195198

Author | Dr. Piero Calvi-Parisetti
Dr. Piero Calvi-Parisetti, a member of Forever Family Foundation's Scientific Advisory Board, works towards the greater good by educating the public about evidence of an afterlife. His constant pursuit for widespread knowledge and understanding of survival of consciousness is shared via a weekly blog on his website is www.drparisetti.com. In addition, he can be reached directly via email at piero@drparisetti.com with matters concerning this workbook and its contents.

Editors | Bob & Phran Ginsberg, Co-Founders, Forever Family Foundation, foreverfamilyfoundation.org

Contributor | Bob Ginsberg

Designer | Ann Shultz, ajsdesigns.net

TABLE OF CONTENTS

LOVE KNOWS NO DEATH

A WORKBOOK FOR TRANSFORMING GRIEF

Chapter 1

Things You Must Know Before You Start

This chapter outlines a few fundamental things about this book, its aims and the approach it follows.

Here you will learn:	• Whom this book is directed to;
	• Why it was written and by whom;
	• What is the basic idea behind it;
	• What this book is and what it is not

HEALING THE PAIN OF A LOSS

The pain of bereavement is universally recognized as one of the most distressing - and yet most common - experiences in life. The loss of a loved one affects different people in different ways. Many, especially at the beginning, experience shock and numbness gradually giving way to overwhelming sadness, with lots of crying. There may be tiredness or exhaustion. Some may feel anger, for example, towards the person who died, their illness or God. Others experience guilt about feeling angry, about something they said or didn't say, or about not being able to stop the loved one from dying. These feelings are all perfectly normal. The negative feelings don't make the bereaved a bad person. Lots of people, for example, feel guilty about their anger, but it's absolutely OK to be angry and to question why. *I have felt little to no anger — only sadness.*

In most cases, with the passing of time and with modalities which are unique to each and every grieving individual, these overwhelming feelings and emotions subside. It is often said that one never completely recovers from the loss of a loved one and the shock of bereavement leaves a "scar on the soul" which will remain forever. Nevertheless, it is a fact that most people who have suffered a loss do go back to living a normal and enjoyable life. They certainly do not forget about their loved one, but they are able to understand their loss as a painful but unavoidable human experience, and gradually move on. *When? How long? How?*

In some cases, though, the negative feelings and emotions do not subside over time. Some people continue to experience intense sorrow and pain at the thought of the loved one, to the point of being able to focus on little else but the loved one's death. This may be accompanied by numbness or detachment,

> if you are in pain over the loss of a loved one, this book is for you

loss of trust in others, irritability or agitation. People in this situation, known by psychologists as *complicated grief*, are unable to enjoy life or think back on positive experiences with the deceased loved one. This is a serious and debilitating condition, which can take a toll on the body as well. The good news is that, with appropriate help and support, even sufferers of complicated grief can make a complete recovery.

THE QUESTION IS: WHAT KIND OF HELP AND SUPPORT?

This workbook is an essential part of the method known as *Love Knows No Death*. In the next chapters you will learn that this method represents an innovative – many would say radical – approach to supporting grief recovery. You will also learn that this method can have a significant positive effect and that it has already helped thousands. Now, it is important for you to understand that, whether your loss is recent or not, whether you feel that you are on the way to recovery or you are still having major difficulties, this project is especially directed at you. The only reason behind the work that has gone into the development of this method is you, your wellbeing, and your recovery. There is no agenda to pursue, no ideology to promote, and no faith to preach. This method only aims to help you to become more proactive *in your own recovery*.

The originator of this method and the principal author of this book is Italian-born, Scottish Dr. Piero Calvi-Parisetti. A medical doctor originally specializing in public health and disaster management, a long-time university professor and a trained psychotherapist, Dr. Parisetti has dedicated over a decade to the study of *applied psychical research*, which is the practical application of the findings of several lines of scientific investigation for the specific benefit of the bereaved and the dying. However, *Love Knows No Death* is far from being a "one man show." This method also brings to you the collective experience of over

Dr. Piero Calvi-Parisetti

10,000 worldwide members and volunteers of Forever Family Foundation, a nonreligious, entirely volunteer not-for-profit organization dedicated to promoting the knowledge of afterlife science and its integration into the grief recovery process. This book is in fact the product of a joint, collaborative effort between Dr. Parisetti and a number of the Foundation's volunteers, who themselves are bereaved people. Many of them contributed with their own testimony and experiences which you will find reported in every chapter where relevant, while others helped by playing the role of editorial board for this project. You may also like to know that nobody got paid for their work on this project, and the modest revenues from the sale of the workbook go directly to Forever Family Foundation to support their charitable activities. *Love Knows No Death* is therefore a 100% not-for-profit initiative.

understanding, not believing

The title of this workbook – which is also the name given to the whole counseling approach – reflects an "unbelievable truth" that we hope you will understand and come to accept. Yes, *love knows no death*. Think for a moment about what those words mean. By that we do not mean that your feelings for your deceased loved one will last as long as you live – that is a self-evident truth that you know about and experience already. No, by that we mean something much more dramatic: your deceased loved one has not vanished nor disappeared into a black nothingness, *and he or she still loves you,* at this very moment. Simply put, the "unbelievable truth" which we'll present to you throughout this book, is that human mind, consciousness, and personality do not end with the death of the physical body. Your deceased loved one is not, in fact, deceased. His or her body has died, but he or she as a person goes on living in a non-material dimension of existence we call the spirit world, for lack of a better term. And, from there, he or she still loves you. *Love knows no death*.

As you go through this book and watch the accompanying videos you will soon appreciate a few fundamental things which are key to this counseling approach. Let us outline them right away so that there are no misunderstandings. **First, we do not have a religious agenda.** We maintain that human personality survives physical death not as a matter of faith, but rather because we have considered the evidence for it. By evidence we mean "the available body of facts or information indicating whether a belief or proposition is true or valid." Like anybody who has taken the time to look at this evidence seriously, and with an open mind, we have drawn our own conclusions. And these conclusions are that, no matter how unbelievable it may appear to you now, *love knows no death*. **Second, since we do not take the unbelievable truth as a matter of faith, we don't expect you to do so either.** This entire approach is based on education, not on preaching. You will be presented with a lot of evidence, including facts, things that happen, and the science spanning investigations and experiments in controlled conditions. You will also learn about the thousands who are in your exact same situations and have directly experienced the unbelievable truth. We'll encourage you to do the thinking, the judging. *You* will draw your own conclusions. You will hopefully come to *understand*, to *realize*, and not simply accept everything based on blind faith.

A rational belief in life after life – that is, a belief based on reason – can help you in many ways. We all know that there is a part of the pain of a loss that is quite simply unavoidable. That is an integral part of our experience as human beings, and there is no therapy, no belief, no understanding that can

> you need to be able to think with clarity

take that away. However, there is another part that *can* be avoided. That is the ultimate pain which comes from thinking that the people we loved and who have passed away have just vanished or disappeared. The thought of death as annihilation is unrealistic, simply because it does not correspond to the evidence – the facts we know about. The pain generated by that, though, is unnecessary. When you will understand – rationally understand – that your loved one has not simply ceased to exist, some of the hopelessness and desperation will go away. When you will realize that, from the spiritual place where he or she lives now, he or she still loves you, then you will open up to the possibility of a contact. Yes, a fleeting, unpredictable, and yet immensely important contact. And, as in the experiences of thousands around the world, if you will be able to integrate this "afterlife perspective" into a healthy grief recovery process, you will truly honor the memory of your loved one, and you will live a better life.

> every person is unique, every situation is unique

Now, before we go any further, it is essential that we point out a few very important things about this method in relation to your particular situation.

This is the most important thing. This method can help you a great deal, but in order to take advantage of it you need to be able to think and reflect with reasonable clarity. If you feel so overwhelmed with grief that you have trouble carrying out your normal routines, can focus on little else than your loved one's death, or if you feel that life has no meaning or purpose, you need direct personal support from a mental health professional before embarking in this course. And, especially, if you have thoughts about taking your own life, you should definitely ask for help. With the right kind of support, you will recover even from what appears as the most desperate situation.

it is okay to war
to feel bette

There is no "prescribed" way to cope with a loss or to react to trauma. There is no "right" or "wrong," there are no "better" or "worse" people in the face of life's difficulties. Do not judge yourself – that is completely unnecessary and makes things even worse. Instead, begin by giving yourself credit for having endured the pain or the fear. That in itself is a difficult and brave thing to do.

IT IS NEVER TOO LATE

Life can be very tough. The death of a loved one is one of the toughest things humans have to go through. Do not add to these difficulties for no reason. Do not think that your natural desire to ease the pain is wrong. Do not think that you "must" suffer in order to show your love. Imagine what your deceased loved one would like you to do: would he or she like to see you continue suffering, or would he or she rather see you gradually improving?

Grief ages very well. Some people heal relatively quickly, but for others the pain of a loss remains almost intact after many years. Do not believe that "it should be over by now." Says who? Who has established how long

this method is n
a quick f

you should suffer? The thought, "If it has lasted this long, it will never go away," has no basis. There is no evidence that people who have suffered for a long time cannot improve. Instead, you may choose to think, "I have suffered for a long time, but I am ready to begin feeling better."

Are you thinking, "It's too soon to begin grief work. I'm not ready yet?" Ask yourself: "Ready for what, exactly?" Not ready yet to feel less bad? Are you listening to yourself? What use do you have for such thoughts? What would you think if somebody told you, "I have cut myself and I am bleeding, but it's too soon to dress the wound. I'm not ready yet?"

In the next chapter you will learn that this method is based on two well-known and proven approaches: patient education and bibliotherapy. Imagine that *bibliotherapy* (self-study of books and the use of self-help manuals) is as effective as a course of psychotherapy in the management of some forms of depression. Therefore, this workbook is a serious resource, and needs to be taken seriously. It can deliver remarkable results, but it requires time and effort. **Do not expect immediate results.** Do not expect that by working through a couple of chapters your pain will magically dissolve. Feeling better is going to be a gradual process. You need time to understand and assimilate the concepts. You will likely proceed in leaps – a little forward, a little backwards, and then a big leap forward, and then a little backwards again. At some point you will realize that the "knot" of your suffering has untied, and you can finally breathe. Then, it is very likely that you will continue improving past that point, as your mind continues processing the concepts and ideas.

You are about to take a very serious educational course. Although we have made efforts to make it as easy to follow and engaging as possible, it will still require your attention and concentration. **Do not expect to be entertained.** This is not daytime television. It is not meant to be

entertaining. You may even find some parts boring. For the first few chapters, you may think that the subjects don't have much to do with your particular situation. Believe us – they do, and it is important that you work through this initial section of the course. And, as we'll explain in the next chapter, this method does not only consist of reading a book and watching videos. You will have to engage personally. You will have to think, to reflect, and to put your thoughts in writing into this workbook. As you commit to this serious work, remind yourself why you are doing this: to be able to reciprocate the love of your deceased loved one, and to heal the pain of your loss.

All video modules for this course are located on the following dedicated page of Forever Family Foundation's website. This link, which can only be accessed by course participants using this workbook, is http://www.foreverfamilyfoundation.org/site/page/65. Please bookmark this page on your computer as you will be using it frequently.

Now, please go to http://www.foreverfamilyfoundation.org/site/page/65 to view Module 1A (10 minutes) and Module 1B (14 minutes) videos

"Learning about the afterlife made me realize his death wasn't the end and there still is a connection between us. This helps and kind of soothes the pain." — AM, Syosset, New York

"Learning about the evidence for an afterlife helps me understand there is a world within our world that energetically is just as vibrant as ours. It takes the fear out of death. It makes one wish sometimes we could bring a bit more heaven into our everyday lives, more love. All that matters is love."
— SB, Boston, Massachusetts

Chapter 2

An Innovative, Effective, Integrated Approach

This chapter describes the overall approach upon which this book is based and the methodology you will follow as you go through it.

Here you will learn:	• How this book is a part of a method which integrates written text, exercises and online videos; How you are encouraged to use it;
	• What psychological theory this method is based on;
	• What you can expect by following it

a workbook ...

The book you hold in your hands is a *workbook*. You may already be familiar with workbooks, as you may have used one in school, or perhaps because you have used one of the many self-help manuals available. In any case, let's briefly recap what a workbook is and how it should be used. A workbook is a paperback textbook containing information that is expected to be understood, reflected upon and somehow learned. Unlike normal textbooks, a workbook is filled with practice problems where the answers can be written directly in the book. In our case, the practice problems will mostly consist of open-ended questions. You will be asked to pause, read a question, reflect for a while and then write a well thought-out answer. This may seem a banal task and, to some, a waste of time. It is absolutely not. We have referred in the previous chapter to medical research concerning the effectiveness of *bibliotherapy* and we said that the use of self-help manuals in cognitive psychotherapy has been demonstrated to be as effective as a full course of sessions with a trained counselor in the treatment of mild and moderate depression. However, the same research clearly indicates that what really makes a difference in the outcomes is that *patients take the time and make the effort of actually doing the exercises in writing*. For some unexplained reason, simply going through the question and answer routine in one's mind is not sufficient. If you want to reap the full benefits of this method, therefore, you will have to be serious, committed, and do the exercises as recommended.

... which seamlessly integrates with video lessons

However, we refer to *Love Knows No Death* as an innovative approach because it is not only based on a self-help manual. In fact, much of the substance – the information we want to share with you on the evidence for life after life – is provided in a series of video lessons. If you have followed the suggestion we gave at the end of last chapter and watched the introductory video, you already have a pretty good idea of how this works. We have created a dedicated page on Forever Family Foundation's website where we have made available the initial 17 videos you will be guided to as you progress through this workbook. In addition, this page has further reading suggestions as well as additional helpful videos you can access. The initial 17 videos are essential to this method. Most of these videos consist of "lessons" produced by Dr. Parisetti, each one lasting between 15 and 30 minutes. Although these lessons are of academic level, they are delivered in a manner that makes them as engaging and easy to follow as possible. The rest of the videos in the program consist of carefully selected excerpts from some of the best documentaries produced during the last 20 years. These are as important as the lessons, as they provide images, stories, and real life examples that support and further explain the information shared in the lessons. So, just as it is essential that you do the exercises as recommended, it is equally essential that you watch the video modules when prompted to do so in this workbook. There will be a fair amount of to-ing and fro-ing between this manual and the videos. This is completely new – it has never been done before in a self-help method. If you follow the instructions, you will soon realize that this is a very powerful approach.

a method grounded in an effective, evidence-based form of psychotherapy

The educational approach of *Love Knows No Death* is grounded in the techniques of cognitive psychotherapy. In the next chapter you will learn more about this form of therapy, because it is important that you fully understand the basis and rationale of what you and we are doing with this method. For the time being, suffice it to say that cognitive therapy has been evaluated by some of the largest research trials in the history of medicine, and, unlike other forms of talk therapy, has been proven to be extraordinarily effective. You will learn that the foundation of this approach – first developed in the 1950s in the US – is very simple: *the way you feel depends entirely on the way you think*. By looking at how the brain is wired, cognitive psychologists noticed that a stimulus is first evaluated by thought, and *then* sent to the emotional centers for the appropriate response. We will present examples and help you realize that exactly the same event can give rise to entirely different moods, depending on the way we look at it.

Research has shown that people suffering from depression have a "negative bias" – their interpretation of events is pathologically distorted. A mass of negative, distorted, unrealistic thoughts intrude constantly into their consciousness. The solution to this problem is simple, and extremely powerful. In cognitive therapy, patients do not learn to "think positively" (that has been proven to have no effect). Rather, they learn how to think "non-negatively." Negative, unrealistic, distorted thoughts are recognized and replaced with more balanced, neutral, realistic ones.

what has this to do with me?"

At this stage you may ask yourself: "What does this have to do with me and my loss?" You may also think, "Of course I am depressed – I have lost a loved one. How could it be any different?" To begin answering these important questions, and to explain what this method is all about, it is now time for *us* to ask you *our* first question and have you reflect on it.

? QUESTION

Would your life, here and now, be any different if you were absolutely convinced that: a) your deceased loved one has not simply vanished out of existence, but that he or she goes on living in a non-material dimension; and b) from that dimension, he or she can still see what goes on in your life, occasionally make some form of contact, and, crucially, still loves you exactly as he or she did before passing?

Please re-read the question and appreciate the details of what is asked. As you reflect on it, please focus on the "absolutely convinced" part. We mean "convinced," not because you would like it to be true, and not because some preacher, guru, holy book or spiritual tradition says so. Imagine that you were convinced because you *know*, because you have looked at the facts, long and hard, and you have concluded that this is how things are: your loved one still exists, love knows no death.

Now, pause for a moment, think about the question, and write a short answer here.

Although we cannot read your answer, it is highly likely that you have said that your life would indeed be different: less painful, less sad, less hopeless. How less depends on individual cases, but the certainty that a deceased loved one still exists is almost guaranteed to heal some of the grief. Now, please turn up your attention to the max, as we are going to say something very important.

Studies on bereavement – as well as the direct experience of millions – show one fundamental thing, which is perhaps the most fundamental concept you will hear in this course. It is so

a part of the pain of bereavement is unavoidable

fundamental, in fact, that it constitutes the very foundation of our entire approach. There is a part of the pain of bereavement that is quite simply unavoidable. It is an essential component of our being human. When a loved one is no longer physically present in our lives, when we cannot see or touch him or her, we are necessarily bound to feel pain. This pain reaction is so deeply rooted that, in fact, even the most evolved animal species show it. You have to understand and accept that nothing – no therapy, no belief, no practice – will ever take that away. Not only would this be impossible, we also think that you wouldn't want it. Not feeling some of the pain of bereavement would mean not being human.

Another part can and should be avoided

However, there is another part of that pain that is avoidable. That part is unnecessary. It hurts you and – as you will learn – it is a cause of much discomfort for your loved one in spirit. When you think that your loved one has simply ceased to exist, you feel unnecessary pain. When you think that he or she has disappeared, vanished into nothingness, you feel unnecessary pain. When you think of death as annihilation of being, you feel unnecessary pain.

Do you remember what we said about thoughts and feelings? *The way you feel depends entirely on the way you think.* Think negative, unrealistic, distorted thoughts and you will inevitably feel bad. This entire method aims to help you understand that the thought "death = disappearance" is unrealistic, **because it is does not correspond to the facts.** When you will understand – *rationally* understand – that your loved one goes on living in a different dimension of existence, that unrealistic thought will go away, taking with it a good part of your pain.

We fully understand that you may be approaching this subject from different "starting points." You may already be convinced – for a variety of reasons – that human personality survives physical death. If this is the

a useful method, no matter where you start from

case, this method may still be helpful to you, as it may provide further substance and structure to your beliefs, reinforcing positive thoughts about your loved one. Or, you may have had some experiences suggestive of after-death communication and don't know what to do with these. Such experiences, you will learn, are extremely common, especially in the first weeks after a loss. You may have experienced a fleeting vision, a touch, a smell, a voice or simply a strong sense of presence. If this is the case, this method will help you to put these experiences into perspective, to understand them for what they really are (your deceased loved one letting you know he or she is still around you) and to help you become open for more in the future. Finally, you may be highly skeptical of the idea of an afterlife. Survival of personality of bodily death may seem to you so utterly unbelievable that you are tempted to simply reject the idea. If this is the case, this method will hopefully help you to see things differently, and to open your mind up to the possibilities. If this is the case for you, please reflect for a moment on what Swiss physicist Raoul Pictet famously said, after having carefully studied the evidence for survival, "I am constrained to believe by the invincible logic of facts."

Now, let's look at a little more practical advice on how to use this method.

1. **Go through the chapters in the given order.** Do not skip around. There is a reason and logic for the modules to have this particular order: please do respect that.

2. **Do not skip chapters.** Some subjects may appear less interesting or appealing, and others more so. Do not give in to the temptation to skip a chapter that looks less interesting. They are all important and they must all be worked through.

3. **If necessary, watch a video again.** The videos accompanying this workbook are not long. Yet, as we said, they contain most of the information we want to share with you. If you feel that you have not understood something, that you haven't gotten the full meaning of what was presented, please do watch the video again. It will be ten or fifteen minutes well spent!

4. **Give time for the information to sink in.** You may be tempted to be as quick as possible in going through the course. Don't. Give your mind the time to properly assimilate the information – the benefits will be greater and more long-lasting. Do not watch more than two modules (or a module and an assignment) per day, and make sure you do your preparations and follow-up as recommended in the relevant chapter(s) of the workbook.

"The evidence confirms my belief that this life is temporary, but our souls are not. I know that I will see my loved ones again, and I am not one bit afraid to die. I might be fearful of the pain and suffering that may come with illness at the end of life, but I am not afraid to leave this life and move on to the next. I look forward to seeing my son, mom, dad, sister, brother, nephew, grandparents…"
— Penny Maroldo, Oberlin, Ohio

"My growing understanding of the abundant afterlife evidence continues to open my mind to the boundlessness of spirit. It has been life-changing. It has helped me to refocus my days on the positive."
— Jim Warren, Salt Lake City, Utah

Chapter 3

Helpful and Less Helpful Approaches

This chapter takes stock of the options a bereaved person has when looking for grief recovery support.	
Here you will learn:	• How many traditional counseling methods are based on an outdated, unsupported model and fail to provide real help;
	• How non-traditional interventions are considerably more successful;
	• How integrating an "afterlife perspective" into the grief recovery process has helped thousands

In Chapter 1 we already highlighted a fundamental fact: every person is unique and every situation is unique. In your specific circumstances, then, this means that *you* are unique and *your grief* is unique. Let us ask you: Do you know of any two people who would react in exactly the same manner to a given event? Of course not – that would be contrary to common sense and experience.

the five stages of grief ... However, when it comes to coping with the loss of a loved one, common wisdom expects us to do exactly that: conform to a rigid, pre-defined pattern. We are almost certain that, even before your bereavement, you heard of the "five stages of grief." This model was first introduced by Swiss Psychiatrist Elisabeth Kübler-Ross in her 1969 book, *On Death and Dying*, and was inspired by her work with terminally ill patients. In the decades since the publication, the Kübler-Ross model gained enormous popularity. Initially developed for helping those facing an impending death, its application was almost automatically extended to those grieving the loss of a loved one. The model is simple, logical and appealing, and so it spread like a cholera epidemic, "infecting" the entire grief counseling profession and expanding into other areas of psychology and sociology to the point that today you even hear about the "five stages of grieving a job loss!"

Too bad the model is not true. The very Dr. Elizabeth Kübler-Ross, towards the end **... in fact do not exist** of her life, openly admitted that this was not a universally applicable model, and that she didn't think everybody had to go through the stages in sequence. And, if you look for scientific evidence supporting that model, you will find precious little. On the contrary, there is ample evidence that the stages of grief in fact do not exist. For instance, George Bonanno, professor of clinical psychology at Columbia University, summarizes his research of more than two decades and involving thousands of subjects by saying that a natural resilience is the main component of grief and trauma reactions and the stages are a myth. A 2000–2003 study of bereaved individuals conducted by Yale University also lends limited support to the stages of grief model, and such model is fiercely contested by the Grief Recovery Institute, which has worked with over 100,000 grieving people during the last 30 years.

traditional counseling is often ineffective Despite this disconcerting lack of evidence, however, the stages of grief model is what you are often offered if you go for counseling. It is assumed that you are the same as the next person and your reactions will necessarily consist of denial, anger, bargaining, depression and acceptance, in this exact sequence. The majority of bereavement counseling interventions aim to help you "work through the stages." And – what a surprise – these interventions are not effective.

In a 2007 scientific paper *(What has become of grief counseling? An evaluation of the empirical foundations of the new pessimism published in Professional Psychology: Research and Practice)*, researchers Larson and Hoyt pointed to the popular yet pessimistic consensus in the grief and bereavement literature that grief counseling was at best ineffective, and at worst harmful to clients seeking help.

Similarly, in a 2008 review of traditional grief treatment outcomes *(The effectiveness of psychotherapeutic interventions for bereaved persons: A comprehensive quantitative review published in the Psychological Bulletin)*, researchers Currier, Neimeyer, and Berman revealed a "discouraging picture for bereavement interventions" which added "little to no benefit beyond the participants' existing resources and the passage of time."

So, it appears that many traditional interventions are based on an unsupported theoretical model and are not helpful. And still, as we said, this is what the majority of grieving people are offered. This is **Non-traditional "afterlife-based" interventions are highly effective** what they get and what they pay for. The good news, however, is that there are a number of non-traditional interventions and experiences that have been repeatedly demonstrated to diminish and, in some cases, even entirely alleviate grief. All of these approaches were introduced or investigated by scientists, medical doctors or mental health professionals and, crucially, they *either imply or are based outright upon the existence of an afterlife*. Let's quickly review some of them, and see what medical research has to say about them.

Dr. Moody's Psychomanteum

Medical reports show that at least half of all persons whose spouse dies report a spontaneous contact from that person after death. Similar reports often come from parents who have lost a child. In general, research indicates that people who have had an experience of after death communication with a deceased loved one, either spontaneously, through a medium or with other techniques, show marked and lasting improvements in their psychological well-being. With this as a backdrop, in the early 1990s Dr. Raymond Moody, a psychiatrist and then Professor of Psychology at West Georgia University, decided to see whether these beneficial experiences of reunion could be replicated outside the haphazard, unpredictable domain of spontaneous apparitions. He developed a technique by which, after an in-depth psychological preparation, the patient sits comfortably for a couple of hours on a recliner chair in a completely darkened meditation room. Dr. Moody named this room "psychomanteum" referencing the Oracle of the Dead in ancient Greece where people traditionally went to make contact with the dead. Behind the chair, a dim light provides a modicum of illumination. From the recliner, all the patient has to do is very calmly gaze into a large mirror, which is placed on a facing wall, in a slightly higher position, so that it does not reflect the image of the patient.

The results he and other researchers obtained went way beyond expectations: a significant proportion of the subjects who underwent this procedure were absolutely convinced that they had an experience of reunion with a deceased loved one. On one point all the researchers agree: success rates in reunion experiences vary, and the nature of the reunion may be very different. The experiences range from a "sense of presence" to voices, smells and touches, all the way up to fully-formed visual images of the deceased talking and interacting as in real life. Most grieving people who go through a psychomanteum experience see their grief substantially reduced and a number of psychological health indicators substantially improved. In her PhD dissertation, for instance, Rebecca J. Mertz demonstrated statistically significant reductions in feelings of anger and guilt, as well as significant increases in positive feelings. The psychomanteum process was commonly described as helpful, healing, comforting, and peaceful. As well, it was frequently reported that the experience left the participant with a sense of well-being and a feeling of serenity and acceptance.

A related but altogether different technique was developed by clinical psychologist Allan L. Botkin, based on a methodology called Eye Movement Desensitization and Reprocessing, or EMDR. Dr. Botkin recounts, "I discovered this effect by accident in 1995 while working with psychologically traumatized combat veterans at a VA hospital. [...] My colleagues and I had been using EMDR for a few years and we had found that we could routinely and rapidly accomplish psychotherapeutic outcomes with EMDR to a degree that we had thought was not possible. In short, we were able to eliminate the reliving component from their memories. I then experimented with a number of variations of EMDR, and I found that a few changes made the standard EMDR technique even more efficient. Once I began incorporating these changes, I was very surprised when about 75% of my patients reported after death communications during the procedure." He gave this technique the name of Induced After-Death Communication, or IADC.

Dr. Botkin's IADC

Based on the experience of literally thousands of cases (Botkin later trained his clinical psychology assistants and the approach was then utilized much more broadly, to the point that several dozen trained therapists now operate around the world), he concludes, "It doesn't matter what you believe, what we believe, or even what the experiencers believe. The IADC experiences we have induced in thousands of patients result in dramatic life changes that heal grief and trauma in a very short time and are sustained long-term. The technique has worth because it works; it doesn't need for us to agree on a belief system or theory about the source of the phenomenon to support it."

remarkable improvements after sitting with a medium Researching the effects of an evidential sitting with a medium may sound a little bit like investigating whether water is wet. After all, obtaining proof of the survival of a loved one as a means to ease the suffering of bereavement is the very reason why people do this. Anybody who has either personally experienced or witnessed after-death communication through a bona fide medium knows how extraordinarily effective this can be in reducing grief. Whether in the privacy of a one-to-one sitting, or during a spiritualist church ceremony, or even in one of the showbiz events we see on television, if the medium is good, legitimate and provides good evidence, people may experience major relief.

But, very interestingly, until recently these effects have never been properly studied scientifically. They were in a way taken for granted, resting on the self-evident reality of people's experiences. It was only in 2010 that this very important subject attracted the attention of serious researchers. Dr. Chad Mosher, Dr. Julie Beischel, and Mark Boccuzzi of the Windbridge Institute carried out an exploratory study showing that – guess what – water is indeed wet!

Using an anonymous survey methodology, 83 participants were asked to retrospectively rate their levels of grief before and after a reading with a medium. As expected, results strongly indicated that participants experience meaningful reductions in levels of grief. The real value of the study, however, lies in the fact that a subset (one third) of participants also worked with a mental health professional (MHP), and were able to draw comparisons between the two approaches.

The participants' verbatim comments about those experiences are extremely telling:

"The medium had a profound effect on my life and my grieving process…. It has helped me in a way I never would have imagined."

"After the reading, I had a different definition of my relationship with my mom that was more special than I could ever expect."

"The medium helped me manage the grief that has been with me for more than 20 years."

"When my first MHP negated the reading I had with a medium, I switched to someone who understood and supported 'my new reality' and therefore received much more constructive help with my grief."

"I only went to a grief counselor for four sessions. I did not continue because I didn't feel that she was helping me either way."

"I know that I personally needed to go through counseling as well. However, the level of healing was accelerated by getting readings."

"The medium reached my heart, the social worker my mind."

Lastly, it is a well-known fact that all those who have had a near death experience (NDE) show dramatic and permanent psychological and behavioral changes. They feel a greater sense of purpose, greater self-acceptance, loss of interest for material achievements and, instead, a tremendous thirst for knowledge for its own sake. Most importantly, the NDE literally demolishes the fear of death completely and forever. While one retains the normal fears associated with the process of dying, the moment of death itself is regarded positively as a liberating transition into a sublime state that NDErs know they have already briefly encountered.

Crucially, however, Dr. Kenneth Ring (a foremost NDE researcher in the 1980s and 1990s) and his colleagues also showed that some of these psychological and behavioral changes show up in people who have only *read* about near-death experiences and who have dedicated some time to their study. The more time that was invested in learning about these experiences, the greater the changes. And not only that - further analysis revealed that the shifts in values and outlook did not fade with the passage of time. In some cases, these persons were describing positive changes that had already lasted two decades.

> *Learning* about NEDs transforms lives as much as *having* an NDE

This captures the entire rationale behind *Love Knows No Death:* We know from research that learning about just NDEs can have such beneficial effects. We believe that, when you will learn that there is solid evidence from another *dozen* fields of investigation pointing to the fact that your deceased loved one goes on living in a non-material dimension, the positive effects will be even stronger.

"Having learned about evidence for an afterlife I don't fear death. I have more patience and love for others and in particular for those closest to me. I am more spiritually guided in my actions, rather than "dogma directed" by many religions. It has helped me living a simpler and more satisfying life." — Susan Donahue, Ashburn, Virginia

"I had very limited understanding of life after death for most of my life. The more I learn about afterlife evidence, the more I want to learn and the more I realize how important it is in this life to be as loving as possible to those with whom I interact." — Lo Anne Mayer, Manchester, New Jersey

Chapter 4

Possible Stumbling Blocks

This chapter describes a few obstacles that may stand in the way of a healthy, rational belief in life after life.

Here you will learn:	• How millions have experiences suggestive of an afterlife, and yet people are afraid to talk about it;
	• The benefits of letting go of unhelpful religious dogmas;
	• How mainstream science ignores and suppresses information about the afterlife

the "workbook plus videos" approach in full swing

This is the first chapter in the workbook in which, following our ground-breaking approach, most of the information will actually be provided by an online video lesson that you are expected to watch. This should not be entirely new to you, as we have already asked you to watch two video modules at the end of Chapter 1. In that case, however, the video modules were an addition, a complement to the written chapter. From now on, when they are used, videos will actually *replace* the written material. The method, once again, is very simple: We will ask you a few questions to begin with, and we expect you to write down the answers here in this workbook. Then, you will spend some 20 minutes watching the online video. Finally, you will come back to the workbook to write down your own thoughts and reflections of what you heard in the video.

Before getting into all that, however, we want to remind you of something very **the "unbelievable truth"** important that you have heard in the first video you watched. Something which the lecturer will refer to again in the video you are about to watch. We called this the "unbelievable truth." It captures the conclusions that can be drawn from an in-depth study of the evidence for life after life. These are the conclusions you yourself are likely to come to. We want to re-state them here, so that you have them fresh in your mind as you watch the video. Please appreciate two things. First, these statements are addressed to you personally just because it makes it easier to understand them. Obviously, their meaning applies just as well to a loved one who may have passed away – they apply to *everybody*. Second, we have tried to encapsulate, in a few simple statements, concepts which are extremely deep and complicated. *Do not take these statements as you would take a revealed religious truth.* In our approach, this "truth" must not be *believed* – it must be *realized* through the study and critical evaluation of the evidence.

- **Your mind, your personality, your consciousness, your memories, all that you identify with yourself, with your feeling of being alive, are not dependent on your functioning physical brain.**

- **When your brain will die, your mind and personality will continue to exist. It will still be you, and it will feel exactly like you, only without a physical body.**

- **You most probably have gone through this transition from the physical to the spiritual world many times already, as this is not likely to be your first incarnation.**

- **After the demise of your physical body, you will spend a certain amount of time in the various levels of the spirit world, and then you will probably, but not necessarily, incarnate again.**

- **In the long term, all this pans out as a project for your own evolution and development. Life, in the material and spiritual worlds, has meaning and purpose.**

Now, before you go on and watch the video, we want you to stop and reflect on three important questions.

The first only applies to you if you are a person of religious faith, or if you follow a particular spiritual tradition. If you are an atheist, or you are simply not interested in religion or in a specific spiritual path, you can safely skip this question and move on to the next one.

? QUESTIONS

Please consider the key concepts and ideas we have expressed in what we called the "unbelievable truth." Do you think, at this stage, that these ideas and concepts are compatible with your religious beliefs or the tradition you follow? Or, do you think that the teachings of your faith may stand in the way of your realization that this is in fact the truth?

Please note your answers below. (If needed, extra space is available on pages 61 and 72.)

The second question has to do not with what you may believe, but with what you or somebody you know and trust may have experienced. *(If needed, extra space is available on pages 61 and 72.)*

Did you ever have an experience (or do you know of somebody who did) which is strongly suggestive of life after life? This would typically be an experience of after-death communication: hearing a voice, smelling a particular perfume or smell, feeling a touch or even seeing the full apparition of a deceased person. This could also include the inexplicable movement of objects and/or bizarre behavior of electrical or mechanical appliances.

If you did have any of these experiences (or you know somebody who did), please briefly describe them below.

If you did not, this is equally meaningful and important for this method. Please describe below your feelings about not having had such experiences.

Love Knows No Death

The third and last question has to do with the way the possibility of an afterlife is dealt with by mainstream media. The question, for reasons that you will understand when you watch the video, is very narrow and precise.

QUESTIONS

?

On the subject of the afterlife, have you seen, heard or read anything in the media other than television programs on "ghost investigators" or sensationalist newspaper articles about alleged spirit possession, paranormal activity, and hauntings?

If you did, this is very important. Please briefly describe what you saw/heard/read.

If you didn't, please reflect on how the subject of afterlife seems to be dealt with by mainstream media, and write down your thoughts.

Now it is time to put the workbook down and watch the video.

Go to http://www.foreverfamilyfoundation.org/site/page/65 to view Module 2 video (18 minutes)

Finally, we would like you to reflect on the three main subjects discussed in the video.

QUESTION

?

RELIGION. This is certainly a sensitive topic and, as stated in the video, we absolutely do not want to challenge any of your existing beliefs. For your own understanding and development process, however, we think it is useful that you reflect on any clash or incompatibility between the conclusions drawn based on the evidence for an afterlife.

Please put your own thoughts and reflections in writing, using the space below. (If needed, extra space is available on pages 61 and 72.)

The direct, personal experience of contact with the spirit world. Whether or not you have had one yourself, what are your reflections about what you learned in the video?

Last, what do you think of the fact that the mainstream media appears literally dominated by the "fundamentalists" of a doctrine called materialism, which maintains that all that exists is matter, that consciousness is the sole product of the activity of the brain and that, when the brain ceases to function, "we" die with it? And what do you think of the fact that scores of top-qualified scientists, who have amassed for a century and a half empirical and scientific evidence to the contrary, have very little access to public information channels and to funding for research?

"While I am a believer, and need no further proof, learning that others are beginning to discover and accept this evidence gives me hope that we all may be more cognizant of our actions in this physical existence."
— MG, Huntington, New York

"Because so many others have had similar experiences, I know that my experiences are not part of my imagination." — Carolyn McMahon, Warwick, Rhode Island

Chapter 5

Thoughts and Emotions

This chapter explains the very basics of Cognitive Behavior Therapy, the most tested and by far the most effective form of psychotherapy, and why it is important to you as a bereaved person.

Here you will learn:	• How the way you feel depends entirely on the way you think;
	• How depression is caused by automatic, distorted, negative thoughts;
	• How, by learning to identify such distorted and negative thoughts, and replacing them with more balanced, realistic ones, even severe depression can lift

essential terminology

Already in Chapter 2 of this workbook we introduced the simple and yet very powerful ideas behind Cognitive Behavior Therapy (or CBT, which is the approach our method is based on). It is now time to go a little more in depth so that you grasp where this form of therapy comes from, what it consists of and what it can do for you. Before we do that, however, we need to be clear about four terms we are going to use quite often. We will try to do that through common language, rather than scientific definitions, so that we are sure we are all on the same page.

By the word **thoughts** we refer to what goes on in your mind. This is the chitchat of ideas that never seems to stop whenever we are awake. Some of these ideas are "verbalized," i.e., they come in the form of sentences (for instance, "What a beautiful day today!"). Many others do not have words associated with them, but, if you wanted, you could easily express them in the form of a sentence.

By the word **emotions** we refer to what goes on in your heart. Not the anatomical heart, but rather the emotional heart. Think of the love you feel for a child, the joy of winning the lottery, the anger for being wronged, or the frustration for not getting something you think you deserved. These are examples of what we call emotions.

By the word **feelings** we refer to what goes on in your body. The sense of chest constriction you may feel when very sad, the racing heartbeat you notice when scared, the tingling in your fingers you may get when shocked, and the abdominal pains you may experience associated with various negative emotions are all examples of what we call feelings.

By the word **behavior** we simply refer to what you do.

Now, at the very core of the revolution brought about by Cognitive Behavior Therapy **the core idea of CBT** (which, from now on, we'll call CBT) lies a new and different understanding of the link between thoughts, emotions, feelings and behavior. This new understanding, pioneered in the 1950s by psychiatrists like Aron Beck and Albert Ellis, is actually very simple. It is phenomenally powerful, however, and it is important that you consider this with great attention.

Beck, Ellis and the other originators of CBT looked at the way the brain is wired and noticed something very interesting and somewhat counter-intuitive: The information coming from the senses is sent first to the centers in the brain which are responsible for interpretation, *then* to the centers responsible for emotions, and *lastly* to the centers which produce a behavior. This happens in a very short time, so we may actually get confused as to what really goes on, but the sequence is clear and inescapable: event, interpretation, emotion, behavior.

Let's make a simple but quite fitting example:

EVENT	INTERPRETATION	EMOTION	BEHAVIOR
I am in the street and I see a hooded person coming towards me with a knife	*I am about to be robbed*	*Fear*	*I run as fast as I can*

Reflect for a moment. It is not difficult, is it? *Before* I feel fear, and obviously before I start running, I have to make sense of what I see. I have to *interpret* the situation or event. From this almost banal consideration emerged the foundation of CBT:

The way we feel and behave depends entirely on the way we think.

This simple but extremely powerful idea is, in fact, not new. Almost 2,500 years ago, in ancient Greece, the philosopher Epictetus formulated the same concept in more eloquent terms:

It is not external events themselves that cause us distress, but the way in which we think about them, our interpretation of their significance. It is our attitudes and reactions that give us trouble. We cannot choose our external circumstances, but we can always choose how we respond to them.

Before we look at the next basic concept of CBT, let's do a simple exercise to make sure that you have fully captured the crucial link between thoughts, emotions and actions. Let's imagine that one night, while asleep in your bed, you are woken up by an unusual noise coming from your living room. The noise is an event, something that happens, and you will agree that the event in itself is neutral, has no negative or positive connotations. Now, using a table like the one above, we will suggest two different interpretations (your first thought about the event).

Please use the available space in the third and fourth columns to describe what you think would be your emotions, and therefore your first reaction.

EVENT	INTERPRETATION	EMOTION	BEHAVIOR
Unusual sound from the living room	*A burglar has entered the house*		

EVENT	INTERPRETATION	EMOTION	BEHAVIOR
Unusual sound from the living room	*The cat has overturned the glass vase, again!*		

As you see, exactly the same event, when interpreted differently, gives rise to completely different emotions, resulting in totally different behaviors. Therefore, once more, the way we feel depends entirely on the way we think.

Based on this simple but powerful idea, the originators of CBT set out to investigate what kind of thoughts people suffering from depression have. What they found shocked them: The minds of depressed patients were literally flooded with *negative, distorted, unrealistic* and *automatic* thoughts.

negative thoughts

Negative thoughts: Depressed people continuously err on the negative side in their interpretation of every situation. Negative events are interpreted catastrophically, and even positive events are turned around and interpreted negatively.

Distorted thoughts: Researchers identified 13 common "cognitive distortions" in the thoughts of depressed people. For example:

All or nothing thinking: The person looks at things in absolute, black and white categories.

Over generalization: The person views a single negative event as a never-ending pattern of defeat.

Emotional reasoning: The person reasons from how he or she feels ("I feel terrible, therefore the situation must really be hopeless").

Jumping to conclusions: A) Mind Reading – the person assumes that people are reacting negatively to him/her when there is no evidence for that; B) Fortune Telling – the person arbitrarily predicts that things will turn out badly.

Unrealistic thoughts: Thoughts which are affected by cognitive distortions are not realistic. They do not correspond to reality.

Automatic thoughts: The dramatic thing about depression is that negative, distorted, unrealistic thoughts fill up the mind *without the person even noticing*. These thoughts are taken for reality, for they are the only thing the person knows.

Negative, distorted, automatic thoughts intruding all the time without the person even noticing? Can you imagine what kind of emotions this situation can generate? It is no surprise that the worst cases of depression lead to the sufferers taking their own life to end the pain.

the answer is not to "think positively" ...

... but rather to learn to think less negatively Once we understand that the root cause of depression is negative thoughts, it may seem obvious that if we wanted to combat the negative emotions we should replace negative thoughts with positive ones. This has been tried, and it did not work. The so-called "power of positive thinking" popularized by pop psychology books, does not in fact exist. It is very important that you understand this. Repeating "everything is beautiful" and "I am the best" until one is blue in the face will not stop the negative thoughts and their associated moods. Furthermore, repeating "everything is beautiful" after, for instance, a personal tragedy is phony and in some way insulting.

The real answer, researchers soon discovered, was to *learn* to *think less negatively*. Cognitive Therapy consists of teaching patients to A) recognize their negative thoughts; B) identify the distortions they contain; and C) replace them with less negative, more balanced, *more realistic* ones. Unlike positive thinking, which sounds phony, *realistic* thoughts are much easier to believe and to take on board. The patient learns to appreciate that less negative thoughts correspond much better to reality.

necessary and unnecessary pain

The CBT approach does not expect that people will feel happy all the time and that they will ignore the negative aspects of unpleasant or traumatic situations. Events, such as the end of a relationship, a financial downturn or the loss of a loved one, are recognized as traumatic experiences that necessarily come with a certain degree of pain and discomfort. CBT aims to eliminate the *unnecessary* part of the pain, which often comes as an unwanted add-on and is supported by unrealistic negative thoughts. To illustrate an example, let's say that Mary's 20-year marriage has ended because her husband has met a younger woman.

results are spectacular

Mary is very sad because she has lost her companion. That is a *fact*, and a considerable measure of sadness and pain are unfortunately to be expected. This is what CBT considers necessary, or unavoidable pain. But then let's imagine that Mary has automatic thoughts like, "He left me because I am a bad person," "the fact that he left me proves that I am unlovable," or "I will never be happy again." Thoughts like these bring the sadness to the level of desperation and shroud the entire situation in utter hopelessness. *That* level of suffering is unnecessary. It is unjustified, because those automatic thoughts are unrealistic. In her pain, Mary forgets all the parts of her life that prove that she is definitely *not* a "bad person." She also does not realize that "bad persons" in fact do not exist, as even those who often act in a bad way have at least some good in them. She thinks she is unlovable, thereby ignoring that she has had many lovers before, that her husband loved her dearly for 20 years, that she has three adoring children and plenty of loving friends. Who's "unlovable" here? Finally, she thinks she can tell the future ("I will never be happy again"). But nobody can tell the future, neither she nor anybody else. When she stops and realizes that is an unrealistic thought, the total, utter hopelessness lifts a little, and opens the way for more balanced thoughts like, "I am very sad now and probably will be sad for a long time. But nobody can predict the future, so I have no way of saying that I will be unhappy forever. In reality, it is at least a possibility that I will be happy again."

This may seem simple, almost banal, but the results of this approach are simply spectacular. Bear with us as we quote some medical research literature. In 1989 researcher Keith Dobson, PhD combined the results of 28 studies carried out by as many universities, concluding that cognitive therapy for depression was superior to pharmacotherapy (anti-depressant drugs) and any other form of psychotherapy. Further studies comparing cognitive therapy for depression with pharmacotherapy specifically have indicated that cognitive therapy is as effective as pharmacotherapy regardless of the severity of the depression. Follow-up studies of the patients treated in the major controlled trials suggest that cognitive therapy of depression is more effective than pharmacotherapy alone in preventing relapse. Responders to cognitive therapy in these studies were only half as likely to relapse or seek further treatment following termination than responders to pharmacotherapy alone.

Now that you have understood that basis of CBT, let us repeat again what we said in Chapter 2 of this workbook concerning the *Love Knows No Death* method and how it applies the concepts and techniques of CBT:

> **a part of the pain of bereavement is unavoidable ...**

Studies on bereavement – as well as the direct experience of millions – show one fundamental thing, which is perhaps the most fundamental concept you will hear in this course. It is so fundamental, in fact, that it constitutes the very foundation of our entire approach. There is a part of the pain of bereavement that is quite simply unavoidable. It is an essential component of our being human. When a loved one is no longer physically present in our lives, when we cannot see or touch him or her, we are necessarily bound to feel pain. This pain reaction is so deeply rooted that, in fact, even the most evolved animal species show it. You have to understand and accept that nothing – no therapy, no belief, no practice – will ever take that away. Not only would this be impossible, we also think that you wouldn't want it. Not feeling some of the pain of bereavement would mean not being human.

> **... another part <u>can</u> and <u>should</u> be avoided**

However, there is another part of that pain that is avoidable. That part is unnecessary. It hurts you and – as you will learn – it is a cause of much discomfort for your loved one in spirit. When you think that your loved one has simply ceased to exist, you feel unnecessary pain. When you think that he or she has disappeared, vanished into nothingness, you feel unnecessary pain. When you think of death as annihilation of being, you feel unnecessary pain. *ALL Correct*

Do you remember what we said about thoughts and feelings? *The way you feel depends entirely on the way you think*. Think negative, unrealistic, distorted thoughts and you will inevitably feel bad. **This entire method aims to help you understand that the thought "death = disappearance" is unrealistic, because it is does not correspond to the facts. When you will understand – rationally understand – that your loved one goes on living in a different dimension of existence, that unrealistic thought will go away, taking with it a good part of your pain.**

Chapter 6

What is it That Dies at Death?

This chapter explains that we are not bodies with a consciousness that we lose at death. Rather, we are consciousness with a body we lose at death.	
Here you will learn:	• How our tendency to identify ourselves with our bodies is just a powerful illusion;
	• What we really fear losing at death are our thoughts, our emotions, our memories, our personality - in a word, our mind;
	• Our mind is in fact independent from the physical brain

With this chapter we enter into the very core of our approach. From now on, there will be no more "framework" issues or introductory remarks. We'll be talking about death of the physical body and survival of mind, consciousness and personality. And, from now on, all the "substance" (the critical information that we expect you to learn and understand), will be delivered through the video modules. The remaining chapters of the workbook will consist almost exclusively of the exercises you are expected to do as part of this method as well as testimony from bereaved people.

Before we can talk about survival, we need to understand death. The information you will hear about in the video module will probably challenge some of the most strongly held assumptions that you – like anybody else – have about death. In fact, we will show you through examples from the medical sciences that our instincts, along with our "common sense" reasoning about our bodies, ourselves, being "alive" and being "dead," may actually be very wrong.

? QUESTIONS

The first thing we need to do, before watching the video, is to assess your current perception of yourself. This is both a simple and a complicated thing. That is, the question is simple but there's no easy way of asking it. The question is something like, "Show me yourself." Or, "Point to something that you identify with your physical self, with your being alive, with your being in the world." Or even, "Point to something others immediately recognize as you." Describe what this "something" is and what it looks like.

your physical self

Please write your answers below. (If needed, extra space is available on pages 61 and 72.)

The second thing we need to do is to investigate your perceptions about your mind. Think about your mental life, your consciousness, your being aware of the world. Think about your memories, your emotions. Think about the continuous chitchat of thoughts that only seems to stop when we are fast asleep. Where is all that located? Where do you instinctively place your mind, your mental self?

Please write your answers below. (If needed, extra space is available on pages 61 and 72.)

Now you can watch the video. After that, please come back to the workbook for one more exercise.

 Go to http://www.foreverfamilyfoundation.org/site/page/65 to view Module 3 video (14 minutes)

In the video you have perhaps learned things that you didn't know, such as the astonishing rate at which different parts of our bodies change. Or, perhaps, you did know such things already, and the video may simply have helped you put this information into perspective. In order for these very important ideas to settle, we ask you now to take some time and reflect on it. Questions that may help you in the process include:

- Did you know how fast and to what extent our bodies change in our daily lives?
- Do you find it difficult to break out of the powerful illusion "you = your body"?
- Can you accept the idea that your mind exists independently from your physical brain?

Based on such reflections, please now write a short paragraph on the theme *The Powerful Illusion*.
(If needed, extra space is available on pages 61 and 72.)

Chapter 7

"Evidence" for Life After Life?

This chapter explains the basis for a belief in life after life based on reason rather than on faith.

Here you will learn:	• What the main sources of information are (anecdotes, investigations and laboratory research);
	• How these sources provide a massive amount of compelling evidence for the fact that human personality goes on existing after the death of the body

This chapter of the workbook, and the video module it is based on, may seem a little challenging for some users of this course. First of all, admittedly, the subjects may come across as boring, theoretical, or uninteresting. If this is the way you feel, it is essential that you "grin and bear it" and maintain a high level of attention throughout the video module. It is not very long, anyway, so your effort doesn't have to be great. The content is absolutely essential, however, and that's why we strongly recommend that you consider it with the greatest attention.

Secondly, some may find it initially difficult to accept that matters typically dealt with as a matter of faith and belief can actually be the object of a critical, rational investigation. Yet, this is exactly the case, and this is in fact what we do in the video module. You will get a "panoramic view" of the many pieces that form the puzzle of evidence in support of the idea of life after life. You will learn that this evidence is not mysterious, arcane, or difficult to find or understand. Masses of evidence are there, ready to be discovered, easily understood and critically challenged by anybody with a will to consider it. You will also understand how very diverse fields of investigation produce results that are in complete accordance with each other, providing "cross-confirmation" and adding to what we call the "collective weight" of the evidence for life after life. At the end of the module, we hope you will have understood that the evidence is far, far superior to what would be required, for instance, in a court of law to convict somebody of murder.

Now, having talked about courts of law, you may have a question: Is there "proof" of an afterlife? This is a very smart question, and in order to answer it – before you get a panoramic view of the evidence – we would like to ask a few questions of you. *(If needed, extra space is available on pages 61 and 72.)*

? QUESTION

Imagine that you find yourself in an open field in the countryside, and that the path you are following is crossed by a deep ditch, maybe a couple of meters (7 feet) wide and over a meter (4 feet) deep. The ditch – a canal, in fact – is filled with murky water, and you have to cross it. Imagine that you find a thick bamboo stick, long enough to span the width of the canal. Do you think that you could walk across the canal by walking on that single stick? Think of the details of what would happen to that stick.

Even if the question sounds banal, please write down your answer below.

Now, imagine that you had five of those sticks, nice and strong, all long enough to span the width of the canal. And imagine you lay them side by side, so that you have sort of a bridge, 30 cm (or about a foot) wide. Do you think that you could walk across the canal by walking on these five sticks? Think of the details of what would happen to that "bridge".

Please write down your answer below.

Finally, imagine that you have 50 of those nice and strong bamboo sticks, as well as some pieces of string to tie them together in bundles of 3 or 5. And imagine that you lay down those bundles side by side to form a bridge one meter (or about three feet) wide. Again, do you think that you could walk across the canal by walking on the 50 strong bamboo sticks? Think of the details of what would happen to that bridge.

Please write down your answer below.

The reason for asking you to answer these apparently banal questions is that the "many sticks" analogy serves as a perfect description of the evidence for life after life. Taken individually, each element of evidence is like a bamboo stick: nice and strong, but – if you really want to be very critical – possibly not strong enough for you to reach the other side of the canal. Take a few of them together, and, with some caution, you would probably be able to cross. Take 50 and bundle them together and you could probably cross the canal in a car!

In this analogy, crossing the canal corresponds to building a rational belief in life after life. As you will learn in the video module, the elements of evidence are not one, five or 50 – there are literally thousands. You will also learn that what we described in the analogy as pieces of string is the fact that these elements of evidence are consistent with each other. Results from research and investigations in diverse and seemingly unrelated fields confirm and reinforce each other, with the result that our "bridge" is in fact more like a six-lane motorway!

The bottom line of all this is that no single element of evidence – no matter how strong and convincing – can be taken as "proof" of an afterlife. It is the collective strength and the internal consistency of an incredible quantity of elements of evidence that justifies a rational belief in life after life.

It is now time for you to watch the video. After that, please do come back to the workbook for some additional reflections.

 Go to http://www.foreverfamilyfoundation.org/site/page/65 to view Module 4 video (13 minutes)

QUESTIONS ?

In order to make sure that the concepts we introduced in the video take firm root in your mind, please spend some ten minutes reflecting on what you have learned. Here are a few questions that may guide your reflections.

- **Did you know that so much empirical and scientific evidence existed for the apparently outlandish claim that mind exists independently from the brain and human personality survives physical death?**

- **Do you understand the difference between anecdotes, investigations and laboratory research?**

- **Do you understand what I mean by saying that the different areas of evidence all point the same direction?**

Finally, one last question: If you were a juror in a courtroom, would you be convinced beyond a reasonable doubt by so much testimony?

Please write down your answer (and the reasons for it) below. (If needed, extra space is available on pages 61 and 72.)

"It [Afterlife science] gives validation to my own experiences and helps me feel connected to a community of others who are having many of the same type of experiences and find hope and peace."
— Rosemary Diaz, Paradise, California

Chapter 8

The Powers of the Mind

This chapter explains that the existence of psychic powers indicates that mind is related to, but independent from, the physical brain.

| Here you will learn: | • How powers like telepathy, remote viewing, precognition and mind over matter have been shown to exist by thousands of strictly controlled scientific experiments; |
| | • How the existence of such powers is incompatible with the idea that the mind is produced by the brain |

This chapter of the workbook and its associated two video modules may at first seem interesting but not related to the situation of a bereaved person. Some of you who are in pain over the loss of a loved one may ask, "Why do I have to learn about such things as telepathy, remote vision, precognition and mind over matter phenomena?" Others may already know a lot about such things, perhaps out of a personal interest. And others still may have had a direct personal experience of what we call "psychic powers."

Whatever your situation may be, we strongly advise you to consider the content of the two video modules with attention. Our strategy is clear: We want to continue chipping away at the idea that "we" as individuals are in fact our brain, and when the brain dies, "we" die with it. As we have seen in a previous chapter, this is a powerful idea, something that we believe instinctively, and something which is constantly repeated by the "experts" we may hear or read about in the media. And yet, no matter how powerful or seemingly popular this idea is, it is actually false. False because evidence says it is false. Anecdotes, investigations and masses of laboratory experiments tell us that mind (our consciousness, our personality, our memories, and our network of affections) cannot be reduced to the activity of the physical brain.

When you will have fully understood that we as humans indeed all have psychic powers and that is one of the proofs that "we" are not our brains, it will become easier for you to accept the idea that "we" survive physical death. When you will understand that the personality of your deceased loved one was not produced by his or her brain, you will open up to the possibility that he or she goes on living in a non-material dimension of existence. And, apart from the specific purpose of this course, learning about psychic powers and the evidence for them can be utterly fascinating.

The first video module associated with this chapter of the workbook is possibly a little "science heavy." Please do your best to understand what is being said and what it means. In order to make all this more interesting, however, we have added a second video module related to psychic powers. It is part of a very well made documentary, and it will show you how some of these powers work in reality.

As usual, before you get to watch the videos, we would like to ask you to answer a few preparatory questions. *(If needed, extra space is available on pages 61 and 72.)*

(If needed, extra space is available on pages 61 and 72.)

? QUESTIONS

Please provide your own definition of "telepathy." It doesn't matter if you don't know exactly what it is at the moment. Please just write a sentence explaining what you understand telepathy to be.

Please do the same with "precognition."

And again, with "psychokinesis" or "mind over matter."

Please reflect for a moment and express your current position as to the existence of these powers. It is important that you are honest now. If you believe they are just a matter of fraud, deception or wishful thinking, please say so.

It is now time for you to watch the two videos. Then please do come back to the workbook for the usual reflection exercises.

Go to http://www.foreverfamilyfoundation.org/site/page/65 to view Module 5 (14 minutes) and Module 5A (11 minutes) videos

The follow-up question we have for you may seem a little tricky. We ask it to make sure that the information – and, especially, its meaning – have really sunk in. Please take your time and consider what is being asked.

? QUESTIONS

Let's imagine for a moment that we were wrong. That, as some "experts" say, mind is nothing more than the activity of the brain. If this were the case please explain the following based on this assumption:

- **How the thoughts present in one person's mind can be transferred to another person's when all known channels of communication are closed;**
- **How people can be conscious of events which have not yet happened;**
- **How thoughts can influence inanimate matter and living organisms at a distance.**

Love Knows No Death

Chapter 9

Deathbed Visions

	With this chapter, we begin addressing the substantial evidence for life after life by describing a very well-known and well-studied phenomenon.	
Here you will learn:	•	That about 10% of people are conscious at the moment of their death;
	•	That, of that 10%, two thirds report visions of what appears as the afterlife, and of deceased relatives, who are said to have come to facilitate their transition;
	•	That there currently is no "normal" explanation that can account for the data

Congratulations! You have endured the most difficult part of the course. So far we've been talking about background, theory, and concepts. Now we begin talking about facts – facts directly related to life after life.

The facts you will hear about in this video module are very well known by anybody who happens to be around dying people, particularly the professionals such as doctors and, especially, nurses. You will learn that this phenomenon is so widespread that nursing schools actually teach their students about it and how to deal with it. The general public, however, is much less aware of what we call "deathbed visions." This is really a shame, because knowing about this phenomenon in itself (regardless of its evident links with all the other elements of evidence for life after life) can have an extraordinary comforting, soothing and healing power.

By learning about deathbed visions you will understand that the moment of death which most of us fear so much (either our own death or the death of a loved one) is in fact, for a great many people, a moment of joy, peace and spiritual transformation. These visions really appear as a "taste" of the spiritual dimension our consciousness is going to move to once our physical body has ceased to function. These experiences suggest that, just before physical death, the "filter" that has forced us to perceive only our limited physical reality is somehow removed, and we become conscious of a non-material reality that's always been around us, without us knowing it.

Crucially, as you will learn, the powerful bonds of love and affection we have built during our lives immediately kick into action as we find ourselves "suspended" between the two dimensions. It is, in fact, our deceased loved ones who come and greet us, welcoming us with open arms into the world to come.

QUESTION

?

Before we go any further, it is important that you assess your own reactions to what you have just read. Perhaps you have heard about deathbed visions. Perhaps you have even witnessed one yourself as you were assisting a dying person. Or perhaps you knew nothing about this phenomenon, and the brief description we have just provided is the only information you have. Whatever your specific circumstances, we would like you to reflect, deeply reflect, on what you think is the true nature of this phenomenon. Do you, at this stage, think that this is "the real thing," that dying people are actually allowed to take a peek into the spirit world they are about to move into? Or do you think that these are most likely fantasies, dreams, or the hallucinations produced by a dying brain? ➜

Please note your thoughts below. *(If needed, extra space is available on pages 61 and 72.)*

Now you can go on and watch Module 6 of the video course. Then, please come back to the workbook for more reflection.

 Go to http://www.foreverfamilyfoundation.org/site/page/65 to view Module 6 video (15 minutes)

QUESTIONS

Did you know that so many dying people have visions of the afterlife just before they die? Did you have any experience yourself, or heard from somebody who had?

How can you explain that people have visions of deceased relatives who they didn't know were dead at the moment they saw them?

Can you think of any other possible explanation, or can we reasonably take these visions for what they appear to be?

"It is helpful for me to know that the relationship with one's loved ones only changes in dynamics but doesn't have to end. It is still difficult in as much as the relationship will never be the same, but that I can call out to them when I need them is a huge comfort." — SW, Tolland, Connecticut

Chapter 10

Near-Death Experiences (I)

This chapter introduces one of the strongest areas of evidence for life after life. After having been resuscitated from a state of clinical death, a large number of people report a life-transforming "hyper-conscious" experience which is common across cultures, languages and traditions.	
Here you will learn:	• What an NDE is;
	• How often NDEs occur and in what situations;
	• What the main components of the experience are;
	• How NDEs completely defy the paradigm that mind is produced by the brain

We are convinced that, nowadays, practically everybody has at least heard of Near-Death Experiences, or NDEs. Since Dr. Raymond Moody published his book, *Life After Life*, in the mid-1970s (which, incidentally, went on to sell over 20 million copies), these incredible life-transforming experiences have gained much popularity with the general public to the point of even becoming the subject of a couple of Hollywood movies.

Therefore, before we even begin getting into the subject at hand, we would like you to self-assess your own level of awareness and understanding.

Please use the space below to answer these questions. *(If needed, extra space is available on pages 61 and 72)*:

? QUESTIONS

Who has an NDE and under what circumstances?

What does a "typical" NDE consist of? What do people who have an NDE experience?

Once you have watched the video module and its accompanying assignment, it will be interesting to check your answers to these questions to see whether you have learned anything new or different.

In the video module, you will hear some striking words from two of the top researchers, Dr. Bruce Greyson and Dr. Pim Van Lommel. Then, you will find a description of the experience – what it is, how many people have it, under which conditions, and what the main common features are. You will learn that all over the world, tens of thousands of people are declared clinically and legally dead for five, ten or twenty minutes, and, after having been resuscitated by medical intervention, report a strikingly consistent conscious experience which changes their life forever. And, in the assignment, you will see and hear from people who actually have had this experience. We are convinced that this testimony in itself may have the power of significantly easing, at least for a moment, your pain or fear.

The subject of NDEs is so crucially important for our approach (and the quantity of information we would like you to absorb and reflect upon) that we have divided the material over three chapters. Please remember that what you are going to learn in the video module and assignment related to this chapter of the workbook is just an introduction. It will give you a somewhat in-depth description of what this phenomenon is, and it may be enough to convince many people of its reality. Others may think that, despite the apparently convincing data and testimony, the fact that people who are clinically and legally dead having conscious experiences highly suggestive of an afterlife may simply be too good to be true. This is why in the following chapters and video modules we will review much more information and invite you to challenge it and to consider any possible alternative explanation. Please remember that the power of our approach depends on you drawing your own conclusions based on the information we provide. As we have been saying from the beginning, we don't want you to "believe" us, or to accept any interpretation of the phenomena we describe without considering possible alternatives. You have to learn, think and understand on your own. That is the way to ease the pain of your loss.

Now you can watch video Module 7 and 7A. Then please return to this workbook for the all-important follow up questions that we would like you to answer before you go on to the next chapter.

 Go to http://www.foreverfamilyfoundation.org/site/page/65 to view Module 7 (12 minutes) and Module 7A (27 minutes) videos

And here are the all-important follow-up questions that we would like you to answer before you go on to further chapters of the workbook. *(If needed, extra space is available on pages 61 and 72.)*

? QUESTION

Drs. Greyson and Van Lommel are just two amongst the top researchers who have studied the subject of NDE for 20, 25 or 30 years. Every one of these scientists and researchers is convinced that NDEs provide strong evidence for life after life. Not one of the people who have spent a lifetime studying the phenomenon questions that. Do you think that these people are crazy? Can they all be misguided? Do they just want to believe?

What do you think about the testimony of the experiencers themselves? Did the NDErs you saw and heard in the assignment come across as mad, delusional, visionaries? Or did they appear reasonable and well-oriented? What does this testimony mean to you personally?

If they had no functioning brain, how is it possible that they were having a conscious experience or any experience at all?

And, how do you explain that not only did they have a conscious experience, but that this experience was so similar for everybody?

"Knowing that our spiritual/metaphysical beliefs that life in some form continues beyond death helped us understand and accept that the car accident was an essential part of our daughter's journey and our journey as well. We focused more on how we could all continue to grow and stay connected and began a more intense, deeper experience of our own lives and purpose." — Lori McDermott, Clinton, Massachusetts

Chapter 11

Near-Death Experiences (II)

	This chapter reviews all the attempts to "explain away" the Near-Death Experience, showing that none of them accounts for the masses of available data.
Here you will learn:	• NDEs are neither fantasies nor projection of religious beliefs;
	• NDEs are very different from hallucinations;
	• NDEs are not caused by lack of oxygen in the brain;
	• NDEs are not caused by drugs or other chemicals;
	• NDEs cannot be explained away as happening just before or just after the state of clinical death

We believe that, after having watched the first two videos lesson about NDEs and its associated assignment, and after completing the exercises in this workbook, most of the users of this method will have experienced at least a glimmer of hope. Taken at face value, the testimony from NDErs and researchers alike seems to leave very few doubts about the central tenet of our approach, the fact that human personality survives physical death.

The NDErs know this because they have personally gone through the experience. They don't believe in life after life – they know that death, as we commonly understand it, does not exist. They have "died," and yet they have continued having conscious experiences, and memories, and affections. They have personally felt that love that knows no death. And, as a result, their lives were radically transformed. It is difficult, we think, not to be deeply moved by their testimony.

And the researchers, on the other hand, who have not lived through such experiences themselves, but have spent a lifetime studying this phenomenon, have unanimously come to the same conclusions. Anybody, absolutely anybody, who has seriously considered the empirical and scientific evidence is convinced that NDEs are strongly suggestive of life after life.

But we know that our readers, with very few exceptions, are not likely to be Near-Death Experiencers or NDE researchers. And we know that old habits (with their associated load of unnecessary suffering) die hard. If you have believed for all your life that death means cessation or disappearance, that belief may be temporarily shaken by what you have learned about NDEs. But then, doubts creep up again. And, with the doubts, the pain of a loss – which may have somewhat lifted when you considered the possibility that your deceased loved is actually still living – comes back with a vengeance.

If this is your case, our strong advice is: Do not take these doubts as your enemy! Take them as your friends! From the very beginning of this workbook, we have been saying that we don't want you to believe us. In this particular case, we don't want you even to believe the NDErs, or the scientists, no matter how convincing their testimony may be. We want you to build a rational belief in life after life, because such a belief, based on reason, is unshakeable. And the benefits it brings with it will last forever.

Therefore, our strong advice is to use the doubts that may have crept in. You have to become convinced, to the best of your understanding, that these doubts have no basis, and that NDEs are in fact what they appear to be.

In this process of critically challenging the evidence, a very important step is to consider what alternative explanations have been proposed to "explain away" NDEs, and to decide whether these "normal explanations" stand up to scrutiny. Your scrutiny. And this is exactly what we are going to do in this chapter and its associated video module.

Before watching the video module, please look at this brief list of "traditional" explanations for NDEs, and indicate, by checking the appropriate box, whether you think they are probably true (that is, they can explain the nature and content of an NDE) or probably false. It's important to do this before watching the video module, in order to check your thinking and beliefs before having reviewed the evidence.

NDES ARE PRODUCED BY:	PROBABLY TRUE	PROBABLY FALSE
Fantasies based on the person's religious beliefs		
Hallucinations in a dying brain		
Lack of oxygen in the brain		
Epileptic fits (seizure) just before death		
Side effects of medication		

Now, if you have checked any of the above explanations as "probably true," please briefly answer this question. *(If needed, extra space is available on pages 61 and 72)*:

QUESTION

?

How do you explain that a person could have a very rich conscious experience (regardless of what causes it) and form detailed memories lasting for a lifetime at a moment when there is no functioning brain?

It is now the time for you to watch Module 8 of the video course. Then, please return to the workbook for a final exercise.

 Now, please go to http://www.foreverfamilyfoundation.org/site/page/65 to view Module 8 video (13 minutes)

QUESTIONS ?

At this stage, it is time for you to pause and take stock of where you find yourself in the process of building a rational belief in life after life. You have learned that the researchers who have studied the phenomenon of NDEs are all convinced that it points to life after life. You have heard from the experiencers themselves. You have learned that the conventional explanations fail to account for the facts. What does this mean for you, personally? Are you beginning to open up to the possibility of life after life?

Please spend a good moment reflecting on what you have learned so far and write down your conclusions. (If needed, extra space is available on pages 61 and 72.)

Love Knows No Death

Chapter 12

Near-Death Experiences (III)

	This chapter explores the out-of-body experience, an extraordinary feature of many NDEs. This strongly suggests that out-of-body experiences are indeed real.	
Here you will learn:	•	During an NDE, many people "leave their bodies" and are conscious of many details about the resuscitation procedure and the environment;
	•	The details of out-of-body experiences have been confirmed as veridical through rigorous investigations;
	•	People born blind appear to see during an NDE

By this time, we believe that even those readers with the most doubts will have "surrendered" to the evidence provided by NDEs for one (already quite extraordinary) fact: People can have conscious experiences and build long term memories while they have no functioning brain. We have looked at such experiences, and we have seen how none of the "normal" explanations can account for what goes on. Accepting the reality of this fact is already very important. As we have been saying from the beginning, understanding that the mind is related to, but independent from, the activity of the physical brain is the first step for building a rational belief in life after life. If all these people had experiences and built memories when they were "dead," then it is most likely that your deceased loved one is still having experiences and building memories. That is – he or she goes on existing.

Our aim with this method, however, is for you to move from "accepting the likelihood" to rationally believing in survival as a fact. We are therefore not ready yet to leave the subject of NDEs. The question we have to address is: Are these experiences "real?" Are they really what they appear to be?

The problem is that even if you are convinced that NDErs have conscious experiences while they are "dead," you may still think that those experiences are like dreams, with no connection to reality. How can we therefore be sure that the minds of NDErs are working just as in a normal waking state while their brains are "out?"

We do so in video Module 9 by looking at two additional and absolutely extraordinary areas of evidence concerning Near-Death Experiences. While module eight was a bit science-heavy, we are happy to tell you that module nine is considerably lighter, as it is mostly made up of sections of TV documentaries. The substance remains extremely important, however, and we ask you to watch the video with great attention.

It is now time for you to watch Module 9 of the video course. Afterwards, please come back to the workbook for some follow-up reflections.

 Go to http://www.foreverfamilyfoundation.org/site/page/65 to view Module 9 video (18 minutes)

(If needed, extra space is available on pages 61 and 72.)

Do you have any "normal" explanation for veridical NDEs?

Do you have any "normal" explanation for the fact that the congenitally blind actually see during an NDE?

Are you ready to accept Near-Death Experiences as one of the areas of evidence pointing to life after life? If not, what are your remaining doubts?

How do you feel, now, if we tell you that there are many other areas of evidence, equally strong if not even stronger?

*"Knowing that life continues helped tremendously. The physical is always missed,
but their essence – their soul – continues."* — MR, Hull, Massachusetts

Chapter 13

Apparitions

This chapter discusses one of the most widespread phenomena suggestive of an afterlife: The fact that people of all cultures - and in all periods of history - report seeing and interacting with apparitions of the deceased.

Here you will learn:	• The frequency, content and common characteristics of apparitions;
	• How "normal" explanations fail to account for the data;
	• How certain apparitions are seen by many people at the same time;
	• How "poltergeists" are a well-investigated and seemingly real phenomenon

In earlier chapters of this workbook we have explained how Near-Death Experiences, in those who have had one, induce a range of profound and beneficial psychological and behavioral changes. We have also noted that these changes are as evident 20 or 25 years after the experience as they are at the beginning. We have also explained that such beneficial changes appear not only in those who have had an NDE, but also in people who have simply read about them, and that the extent of those changes is proportional to the time and effort put into the study of NDEs. We have repeatedly said that this is one of the pillars behind our "afterlife education" approach: Knowing about and understanding the masses of evidence for life after life has a major transformative power that can be very helpful to those mourning a loss.

Now, what about other paranormal and spiritual experiences? The question is relevant, because in the video module you will learn that a significant portion (in fact, the majority) of the general population reports having seen apparitions. A large percentage of American adults, for instance, declare to have had some form of contact with a deceased person. Such kinds of experiences are defined in psychology as Spiritually Transformative Experiences or STEs. Do STEs have the same beneficial effects as Near-Death Experiences? You bet!

A study by researchers J. F. Kennedy and Dr. H. Kanthamani, for instance, shows that these experiences increase interest and beliefs in spiritual matters and also increase their sense of well-being. More specifically, the majority of participants in the study reported the following: Increased belief in life after death, Belief that their lives are guided or watched over by a higher force or being, Interest in spiritual or religious matters, and A sense of connection to others. And, especially important for somebody grieving a loss, Spiritually Transformative Experiences (STEs) induce greater happiness, well-being, confidence, and optimism about the future. More importantly, STE's decrease the fear of death, depression, anxiety, isolation, loneliness, as well as worry and fears about the future.

Interestingly, 45% of the respondents indicated that a paranormal experience had made them very afraid. However, this fear appeared to be temporary or mixed with positive feeling as only 9% indicated that their experiences have been scary with no positive value.

Similar results were found by a range of other scientific studies, all pointing to the fact that anomalous experiences indeed promote well-being and spirituality. We are therefore convinced that dedicating some time to the study of these phenomena can have similar beneficial effects.

Now, if you belong to the lucky majority of people who have "seen a ghost," or have had other experiences suggestive of life after life, you know all such things by direct experience. If, on the other hand, you have never had such an experience, or you have had one but have doubts about it, video Module 10 and its associated assignment will help you understand.

Module 10 is somewhat atypical, as it asks you, the viewer, a number of the questions that would normally be asked here in this workbook to prepare you to watch the associated video assignment, Module 10A. This video is an extraordinary documentary on a scientific investigation of a well-known poltergeist case in the United Kingdom. Please do carefully take note of these questions. Watch the documentary with these questions in mind. That will assist you in being more critical, and understanding better. Then, you will be required to answer them in writing in the workbook after watching the two videos. *(If needed, extra space is available on pages 61 and 72.)*

You can now watch Module 10 and Module 10A videos. After that, please return to the workbook.

 Go to http://www.foreverfamilyfoundation.org/site/page/65 to view Module 10 (11 minutes) and Module 10A (12 minutes) videos

QUESTIONS

?

Do you think that the events described in the documentary and attributed to "Pete" can really be only a matter of "imagining things"? Please explain your thinking.

Do you think that the entire thing might be explained by fraud? What would be the reason or the motive for them to mount such an elaborate hoax?

Given the phenomena described in the documentary, do you think that such a hoax is even technically possible?

If this were a hoax, what do the independent witnesses stand to gain in participating in the fraud?

Professor Fontana was convinced of the paranormal nature of the phenomenon. Can a reputable academic, who also is a careful, experienced investigator, get it so totally wrong?

If this were not a hoax, and Professor Fontana was right in believing that the spirit of a deceased boy was behind the phenomena, what does this tell you about life after life?

"My after-death communication experiences have lessened my grief and filled me with love and hope. They have helped me enormously with the grieving process. They continue to happen on a regular basis and are a part of my life now – experiences that I look forward to. They always lift my spirit and fill me with happiness and wonder." — Ann Savino, Alameda, California

Chapter 14

Mediumship (I)

This chapter introduces the strongest area of evidence for life after life: communication with discarnate personalities through gifted mediums.

Here you will learn:	• How mediumistic communication happens on a broad spectrum, from the useless to the sublime;
	• How it is virtually impossible that, in good readings, mediums provide information by simply guessing

In our systematic review of areas of evidence for life after life, we have now come to what is certainly the most important: communication with what we call "discarnate personalities" through a gifted medium. So important it is, in fact, that a good, evidential sitting with a medium can be the one defining experience that is enough to convince many bereaved people that their loved ones have not disappeared, and from the spirit world they inhabit, they still love us and care about us. You will remember that we have seen, in Chapter 3, how scientific research shows that an evidential sitting with a gifted medium can lead not only to significant reductions in the pain of grief and improvements in overall psychological health, but is often rated by those who have had one as vastly superior – in terms of benefits – compared to traditional counseling or psychotherapy. The bottom line of all this is that both research and the testimony of countless bereaved persons (as captured by the quotes you find in the boxes throughout these pages) confirm that a good sitting with a medium can have extraordinary effects.

However, we know that there are several obstacles that may stand in the way of this defining experience. First of all, some may be reluctant to consult a medium – either because of religious prejudices or for fear of falling prey to a dishonest fraudster – and therefore deprive themselves of the potentially healing effects of such experiences. Secondly, good mediums are rare, unfortunately.

Let us make ourselves very clear here. We know that the world of mediums includes nasty people who will try to prey on fragile personalities like the bereaved and pretend to communicate with the spirit world while in reality employing conjuror tricks. However, our in-depth knowledge of this world tells us that these cases are rare. We believe that the vast majority of people who call themselves a medium are honest and well-intentioned and truly have a desire to help. The problem with many of these people, however, is that their skills are modest. Although it appears that mediumship can to some extent be developed, it is clear that the core skills (the "gift" of mediumship) are innate – you either have it or don't. And, as we said, truly gifted mediums are rare. Therefore, some of you may have had sittings with modestly skilled mediums, and came away with more doubts than certainties, and with no reduction on the levels of grief. Thirdly, and finally, some of you may have had a really good, evidential sitting with a medium, and still doubt the experience. "Was it real?" "Did I just imagine things?" "Was the medium simply guessing?" "Did I read more into what was actually said by the medium?" Such doubts have the power to demolish even the best experience and, obviously, to impede any positive effects.

If your problem is finding your way to a good medium in a world which is unchartered territory for you, Forever Family Foundation has a great resource that may help you a good deal.

What You Need to Know Before, During and After a Session With a Medium (page 62)
This addendum, included at the end of this workbook, is a complete reproduction of a booklet produced by Forever Family Foundation that addresses commonly asked questions about Mediums and the process of Mediumship.

An additional resource on Forever Family Foundation's website is a complete list of mediums who have been evaluated for mediumistic proficiency and certified by the foundation. The link to this resource is: http://www.foreverfamilyfoundation.org/site/certified_mediums.

However, as part of our mission to help you develop a healthy, rational belief in life after life, our main aim with this chapter and the two following ones is to validate any good experience you may have had – and still doubt – and to chip away at any misgivings you may have based on incomplete or incorrect information about mediumship. To do so, in video Module 10, instead of providing much theory, we attack the subject of mediums directly by looking at a séance of extraordinary British medium Gordon Smith, filmed by the BBC. Gordon is as gifted a medium as they come. He has been in operation for almost three decades now, helping thousands of bereaved people and astonishing large audiences with a level of skill that is difficult to describe to somebody who has not witnessed it.

Therefore, this is exactly what we are going to do. We are going to see Gordon in action, filmed in real time as he talks to a bereaved couple who have lost a son. This is such an intense and humanly enriching piece of television that watching it can be a very uplifting experience in itself. However, since we want to provide material for you to reflect upon, we will engage in a fascinating thought experiment. In the next video, we critically "dissect" the séance with a method called "reverse probabilities," to conclude that it is fantastically unlikely that the medium got all the information correct by simply guessing.

Watch the module with particular attention, for it is one of the most important in the entire series, and then come back to the workbook for some essential follow-up questions.

Go to http://www.foreverfamilyfoundation.org/site/page/65 to view Module 11 video (19 minutes)

What does your heart tell you about the séance of Gordon Smith?

? QUESTION

What does your mind tell you about our thought experiment?

Can you think of any "normal" way Gordon could have acquired such precise, detailed information?

"When my partner died, I wanted very much to be in contact. Eventually I found the right medium to work with, and it was absolutely wonderful. I came away knowing that love never dies, and my partner is and always will be available for me."— KW, Belchertown, Massachusetts

Chapter 15

Mediumship (II)

This chapter describes a range of scientific experiments indicating that mediums indeed talk to the dead.

Here you will learn:	• How different experimental protocols have been developed to rule out the possibility of the medium "fishing" and "cold reading" the sitter;
	• How to make sure that the information provided by the medium is recognized as specific, relevant and accurate by sitters

For many bereaved persons, the only consolation is the belief that a deceased loved one goes on living in a non-material dimension of existence. As you know, our aim with this method is to demonstrate that such a belief is not a matter of blind faith or wishful thinking, but can be entertained by a rational person based on masses of compelling evidence. Showing that the automatic thought, "death = annihilation/utter disappearance" is, in fact, not true, does not fill the void left by the loved one's passing, but removes at least one significant layer of suffering and hopelessness with remarkable positive results for the bereaved.

However, it is one thing to be rationally convinced of the survival of consciousness and personality of bodily death based on the study of the available evidence. Quite another thing is knowing, based on direct, personal experience. For thousands of people all around the world, such direct knowledge comes through the services of a gifted medium. From the perspective of the sitter (the bereaved person), an evidential sitting with a medium amounts to living proof. He or she will not need anything else. The rest of us will have to rely, once again, on reason. A big question then begs to be asked, "Do mediums really talk to the dead?"

The short answer is yes.

The long answer, if you want to satisfy your reason and rationality, is a lot longer. In video Module 12 and 12A, we will summarize the methodology and results of the research that has brought mediumship research into the laboratory.

Confronted with a claim as preposterous as communicating with disincarnate personalities, our rational mind would come up with at least three key questions:

First: Are the statements by the mediums precise, focused and specific enough to actually mean something to the "sitter" (the person who consults the medium to contact a deceased loved one)? This is the criticism typically leveled by skeptics who claim that statements by the mediums are intentionally vague, so that anybody – especially a bereaved person – can read something into them.

Second: If the statements are indeed specific and meaningful, can mediums deliver them without any previous knowledge about the disincarnates or sitters, in absence of any sensory feedback, and without using fraud or deception? There is no need to say that these are the "weapons" used by the skeptics to try to discredit what we technically define as Anomalous Information Reception (AIR).

Third, and finally: If AIR actually takes place (which in itself is most extraordinary and fascinating), does this information actually come from disincarnate personalities? Observers of this phenomenon have proposed that such information may be "read" by the medium from the mind of the sitter, or from some sort of "memory" embedded in the fabric of space-time.

To answer these key questions, psychical researchers have employed the most sophisticated investigation techniques dating back to the end of the 19th century. Through exquisitely refined research protocols and with the most rigorous controls, "historical" researchers have undoubtedly answered "yes" to all the three questions. However, this was "field" research – observing and trying to understand a phenomenon as it happens in its natural environment. It was not until the late 1980s that mediumship research had been brought into the laboratory, an environment in which investigators have control of most – if not all – the variables of the process, and can perform quantitative, statistical analysis on the results, as it happens in any other branch of science.

Don't worry if all this sounds a little confusing at this stage. Do watch video Module 12 now, which explains why it was necessary to bring the process of mediumship under the strict scrutiny of scientific research. And, immediately after, watch the assignment for Module 12A. This is a documentary showing you how this research is actually done. You will see the actual research mediums in action, and marvel at the level of detail in the communication.

Then, as customary, please return to the workbook for a few follow-up questions. (If needed, extra space is available on pages 61 and 72.)

 Go to http://www.foreverfamilyfoundation.org/site/page/65 to view Module 12 (12 minutes) and Module 12A (8 minutes) videos

? QUESTIONS

What did you think of mediums before watching these modules?

Can you explain the difference between mediums and psychics?

Did you think most mediums were frauds?

Have you changed your mind based on the information provided in the video modules?

"I realized that the soul lives on forever and I can access loved ones in heaven. I have healed and gone through phases of grief sooner than most do. I miss them physically but I know they are not missing out on milestone events."
— PN, Holtsville, New York

Chapter 16

Mediumship (III)

This chapter describes the phenomenon of so-called "drop-in communicators," which provides further evidence that human personality survives physical death.	
Here you will learn:	• What "drop-in communicators" are;
	• Why they are so important in confirming the survival hypothesis

After studying and critically reviewing the information presented in the last two chapters, we believe that it would be very difficult to discount communications received from the spirit world through mediums as the product of fraud or deception. Equally difficult would be, we think, to take them as anything other than what they appear to be: messages from discarnate personalities – people who were once alive on earth and now are alive in a non-material dimension of existence. Becoming convinced of this reality is essential – we keep on saying – for two reasons.

Firstly, if you understand that those who speak to us through mediums are indeed "spirits," you will understand that your own deceased loved one has not disappeared, and that he or she is still very much present in your life even if you cannot see or touch him/her. This is very important, and we ask you to reflect on this for a moment.

Just considering the modern times, we've been receiving messages from the spirit world for over 150 years (in fact, these kinds of messages have been reported since the dawn of times). These communications in themselves have an extraordinary healing power, because, as we just said, they are an indication that death as we commonly understand it does not exist. However, the importance of these messages becomes even greater – immeasurably greater, in fact – when you consider what the spirit communicators have constantly and consistently been telling us. They not only show general awareness and consciousness, they show awareness of our lives - awareness of what goes on this very moment in the material world they left behind. And they show intentionality: our deceased loved ones have wishes and desires just like as they did when they were in a physical body. They keep telling us that they still love us. Love knows no death!

Secondly, perhaps you have considered going to see a medium in the past, or are considering it now, and what held you back was that you were not sure whether any message you may receive would originate from your deceased loved one. Or perhaps you have had a sitting with a medium and still are somehow unconvinced, even in the face of very evidential messages. If this is the case, please carefully consider the following:

1. We do not claim that all communications received from mediums are the real thing. Mediumship is a highly unevenly distributed gift, and many people calling themselves mediums may actually delude themselves and others. Please refer to the addendum at the end of this workbook, *What You Need to Know Before, During and After a Session with a Medium (page 62)*.

2. Communications received from gifted mediums, however, are the real thing. They have been shown to considerably alleviate grief. The more you are rationally convinced that they are messages from your deceased loved one, the greater the psychological benefits you can reap from a sitting with a good medium.

The last video module dedicated to mediumship is therefore intended to iron out any residual doubt you may have concerning spirit communication. It is an anecdote – no heavy science stuff – and as such it will be easy to follow. The subject is "drop-in" communicators – discarnate personalities who show up at séances, unbeknown to anybody, and give evidential details which are later investigated and found to be true. In particular, this is the extraordinary story of medium Eileen Garrett and a very famous – and much investigated – drop-in communicator.

Please watch the video with attention, and then come back to the workbook for some follow-up questions.

 Go to http://www.foreverfamilyfoundation.org/site/page/65 to view Module 13 video (17 minutes)

Go to http://www.foreverfamilyfoundation.org/site/page/65 to view Module 13 video (17 minutes)

? QUESTIONS

What do you make of the R101 story?

Can this be a fabrication?

What explanation can you possibly think of for drop-in communicators?

Do they provide further indication of survival of personality to bodily death?

Love Knows No Death

Chapter 17
Instrumental Trans-Communication (ITC)

	This final chapter introduces one of the strongest areas of evidence for life after life: communications received from (and, in some cases, transmitted to...) discarnate personalities using technological means.
Here you will learn:	• How, for more than 60 years, the voices of the deceased have appeared on tape recorders under conditions that rule out any "normal" explanation;
	• How such voices are also heard through radio receivers and telephone calls, and images are even received on television;
	• How the usual skeptical explanations fail to account for the results of many decades of research and investigations

The area of Instrumental Trans-Communication (ITC) is unfortunately fraught with misunderstanding and confusion. The results of "experiments" are often misunderstood by scores of people who simply want to believe, and in many cases such experiments are just crude attempts by untrained, unscrupulous hobbyists to produce "something" paranormal. It is therefore essential that you fully understand how this activity by scores of amateurs differs from the serious science and robust evidence provided by ITC.

It is no mystery that we live in a highly technological world. In fact, we have been doing so already for several decades. It should be no surprise, therefore, that our loved ones in the spirit world try – successfully, in many cases – to use our omnipresent technology to send us their messages of love. As is the case for other forms of after-death communication, we don't even begin to have an explanation for just how they manage to do so, but the fact is that – as you will soon learn – the proof of such communication is incontrovertible. However, while technology is overabundant all around us, real after-death communication through technological means is relatively rare. Now, the problem is that there are scores – literally tens of thousands – of people who have taken up trying to communicate with the dead through technology as a hobby. Practically every town in the US, for instance, has its own "paranormal investigation group," and one of the typical activities of such groups are "vigils" in which, armed with tape recorders, these enthusiasts roam around graveyards or places which are supposed to be haunted and try to record the voices of the dead. The results of such activities are generally nil. The tape recorders record just ambient noise, fragments of conversation and perfectly natural sounds. The problem is that, pushed by their own desire to believe they have caught something on tape and by a sort of "competition" with other groups, these amateurs imagine that they are hearing something in the noise on tape. The Internet is awash with websites in which such groups publish their "results," and listening to these recordings is generally a depressing exercise: nobody can hear even a fraction of what was allegedly caught on tape.

Now, for a complete change of scenario, we want to introduce the last video in our series. This, unlike the previous ones, is not a lesson by Dr. Parisetti. It is an absolutely extraordinary documentary called *Calling Earth* by producer Dan Drasin. These riveting 95 minutes will teach you all there is to know about real Instrumental Trans-Communication. You will hear interviews with the real researchers – experts, scientists and academics – who have, over the course of the years, amassed amazing quantities of extraordinary evidence. You will hear plenty of examples of what are technically known as "Class A Voices" - recordings in which the anomalous voices are clearly understandable by anybody who listens to them. And, when you will learn about the experimental conditions under which these voices were obtained, you will marvel.

Calling Earth, therefore, is extremely important to separate the real ITC evidence from the delusion of masses of amateurs. However, as you will watch this excellent movie, you will appreciate something more profound, and immensely more important. Yes – by learning about the controlled experiments and the useless "normal" explanations, you will indeed surrender to the fact that these voices (and images…) are indeed paranormal, and that they most likely come from deceased people in the spirit world. In addition, you will soon realize, listening to what the voices are saying, that our deceased loved ones remain connected with our material world. Even if we cannot see them and touch them as we used to do when they were in our physical reality, they are present in our everyday life. They are aware of what goes on in our lives, they remain engaged. This is exactly the same message we get from them through the help of gifted mediums, only, in this case, we get the message directly from them: from wherever they are, they still love us!

Now, please watch the video. Keep in mind that it is longer than the ones you've watched so far, so make sure you have the time. Also, this is such a great production – so packed with information, and yet quite riveting and easy to follow – that you may want to watch it together with friends or family members who are not necessarily familiar with the idea of evidence for life after life – it makes for a fantastic introduction!

Then, please come back to the workbook for the final exercise.

 Go to http://www.foreverfamilyfoundation.org/site/page/65 to view "Calling Earth" (95 minutes)

QUESTION

Please write a short essay on the subject of technology and after-death communication. Note any experience you may have had yourself, or heard of from others. Write about your understanding of the phenomenon before and after watching *Calling Earth*. Reflect on the deep meaning of the messages we receive through tape recorders, radio receivers, telephones and television. *(If needed, extra space is available on pages 61 and 72.)*

"It [After-death communication] lessened the pain. You always wonder if they are OK. Signs from them answer that question." — JH, Las Vegas, Nevada

Chapter 18

Bringing it all together

A word from Robert Ginsberg, Vice-President of Forever Family Foundation

There have been countless "self-help" books written about grief, most of them guiding the reader through various stages of bereavement, advising what to expect, and how to cope. As a bereaved parent, I read about twenty such books and found no solace from my profound sadness and horror. What I read were simply words put on paper by people who I believed did not have a clue as to what I was feeling. Bear in mind that authors are writing based upon their own belief systems and training, and any cookie cutter approach to such a topic is fraught with peril.

Let's face it, there is only one thing that can have a dramatic effect on the grief transformation process for those who suffer the loss of a loved one . . . the knowledge that they still survive. By survive I am not referring to some vague faith based notion that they live on in our hearts or sit strumming harps on clouds in the heavens. I am suggesting the evidence-based reality that our minds (consciousness or soul if you prefer) simply transition to life in a non-physical realm.

I know that for most of us, this knowledge is hard to grasp in view of the materialist indoctrinations instilled in us by our educators, scientists, medical professionals, media and other influences. Before co-founding Forever Family Foundation, I was entrenched in these same beliefs and thought the suggestion of an afterlife to be preposterous and nothing more than fantasy. The death of my daughter shattered my world; my existence in it seemed meaningless; and I envisioned no possible respite from my grief other than my own physical demise. I eventually progressed from denial, to hope, to belief and ultimately, to knowing that we are more than our physical bodies. The information that I have learned over the years is accessible to all who seek it, as so many members of Forever Family Foundation have already discovered.

The first step to grief recovery, in my opinion, is to put preconceived notions aside and commit oneself to integrating an "afterlife perspective" into thought process. Simply put, this means keeping an open mind and making a sincere effort to learn about the evidence that we survive physical death. This is vitally important and you must remain focused as there may be obstacles along the way. Friends, family, and mental health professionals might tell you that such thinking is grief driven and is counterproductive to your transformation. Clergy might advise that the afterlife is exclusively part of religious domain and depends upon obedience to certain rules and dogma. In addition, your own ego and grief might try to take over, leading you to second guess yourself.

It is often said by people in deep grief that life as they knew it is over, and the person they once were no longer exists. I certainly once felt the same way. However, I took a cue from the innocence of children as I navigated my "new life." Some readers may be aware, either from personal experience or knowledge of research, that babies and young children have the same afterlife encounters reported by adults. The difference lies in the fact that children have no basis by which to judge or interpret. Everything they experience is "normal" and they simply relate what they experience. I made a conscious effort to set my baggage aside and simply took what I experienced and learned at face value. I believe that this is something that all who search for answers should incorporate into their personal exploration.

Always keep the ultimate goal in mind. If you should become convinced by the evidence that your loved one survives, envision how differently you would feel knowing that death is merely stepping through a doorway into another room.

A good place to start is by learning about such things as telepathy, intuition, remote viewing, distant healing and other phenomena that show that our minds can act independently of our brains. If our minds are different from our brains, can extend beyond our skulls, and transcend time and space, surviving death becomes not only possible but logical. You have read about such evidence in this workbook, but a simple internet search will lead you to many great books about these subjects from well credentialed scientists.

Along the way, always remain open to the possibility that you are capable of receiving some form of after death communication. I made this mistake for several years as I continuously attributed extraordinary occurrences to coincidence. If you are not open enough to recognize such signs and communications, or automatically dismiss them, important personal evidence is missed. Such encounters might take the form of dream visits, physical manifestations, electronic voice phenomena, synchronicities, apparitions, or other signs that non-physical encounters are taking place. If you should be fortunate enough to receive such a communication, always write it down in a journal for further reference.

You Are Not Crazy
For years foundation members have been telling us that, in addition to outside influences, their own reasoning tells them that they are crazy for believing that the dead can communicate, or even exist for that matter. This feeling is reinforced by the fact that few people share their other worldly experiences, nor do they openly discuss the scientific evidence of which they have become aware. Why wouldn't you think you were nuts if you thought that you were the only person with such thoughts? The fact is, people around the globe have been reporting these experiences for centuries, and the scientific evidence, although often suppressed, is so overwhelming that it is beyond question. It is not surprising that people will only share such experiences when they feel that they will not be labeled or judged. Forever Family Foundation has hosted Afterlife Discussion Groups throughout the U.S. for many years. These are small gatherings of people who wish to learn about the established evidence and share experiences. It never ceases to amaze me how many people, once they feel comfortable with other group members and the facilitator, start sharing fascinating experiences that they have previously kept hidden. Foundation members consistently tell us that one of the best benefits of the organization is simply the knowledge that they are not alone, and most certainly not crazy!

You Are Not Disconnected
What contributes to grief is the belief in the finality of death. In a world where just about anything is possible, death seems to be the one event for which there is no solution. I remember people coming up to me after my daughter's passing and asking if there was anything that they could do for me. I know that they meant

well, but the query seemed inane and hurtful. My answer was always something like, "What I want you cannot provide." Once I came to grips with the fact that I was not going to get her back in the physical, my mission became finding out if it was theoretically possible that her essence still survived, and if so, was there any credible evidence to support it? As I learned about the staggering evidence developed from laboratory and field research, combined with the centuries of anecdotal evidence, my heart lightened. While a grief therapist tried to encourage me to disconnect from my daughter and get on with my life, my logic and instinct told me that the relationship was far from over and should be embraced. The name of our organization, Forever Family Foundation, signifies how the bonds of a family do not end with physical death.

What if our deceased loved ones remain a part of our life, as the evidence clearly suggests? That means that they are not only aware of our grief, but feel our pain and sorrow. I used to think about this often, and suggest you do the same. Even though they, with their new perspective in the spirit world, know that there is no such thing as death, surely it must affect them in some way. Why else would they spend so much time, at least initially, in getting messages to us proving that they still exist? It is to lessen our grief and provide insight into the nature of the universe. Also, let's take a practical view of things. Let's assume that you believe that death is final, miss your loved one terribly, and wallow in your grief for the rest of your physical life. Eventually your time comes to physically die, and then you find yourself very much alive in new surroundings. Do you think that your thought might be, "Crap, why did I just waste thirty years in the physical feeling sorry for myself?" Mine certainly would.

Afterlife Evidence Can Be Life Changing

Once you become familiar with the research involving near death experiences, deathbed visions, mediumship, reincarnation, apparitions, electronic voice phenomena, after death encounters and other phenomena, it is extremely difficult to dismiss the implications. One could take a specific area of research and try to dismiss the evidence as an anomaly. However, when you consider all of the evidence as a whole, there is only one logical conclusion to be made. The knowledge that physical death is by no means final and that our loved ones remain conscious and part of our lives most often provides a lifeline and allows those in grief to lead meaningful and productive lives.

Dos and Don'ts

Although many will tell you otherwise, there aren't any rules. Grief has no set timetable, the stages people talk about are often out of order or non-existent, and every single person will grieve in their own way. I have encountered many people who actually become defined by their grief. These people are most often not open to the possibility that their deceased loved one still survives, and may even take offense to the very suggestion as if it somehow would diminish their grief. Grief is complicated. I remember the first time that I laughed after my daughter's death and subsequently felt immediate guilt. How dare I laugh? I interpreted the action as being disrespectful and not showing the proper remorse for someone I loved and adored. Others find comfort in speaking about their deceased loved one and laughing as they reminisce. I remember not being able to walk into my daughter's room for many years, as it was simply too painful. Others find solace in spending as much time in their loved one's room and surrounding themselves with personal belongings. My point is that everyone will react differently. Those who grieve should do not what others do or advise, but whatever they feel is right for them at the time. The good news is that things change once we learn, explore, and experience.

Caution should be exercised by the bereaved in certain areas, as there are unfortunately many people who look upon those in grief as prey. I have come across countless numbers of people who were shaken down by unscrupulous and deceptive practitioners acting under the guise of being an evidential psychic medium. I have seen intelligent professional people, so desperate to contact a deceased loved one that they have shelled out thousands of dollars for things like "curse cleansing candles." There are many legitimate mediums in practice today (some certified by Forever Family Foundation) that can do what they claim. However, I would estimate that somewhere between 85-90% of all people claiming to be mediums are inexperienced and not evidential, deceptive, or even fraudulent.

The afterlife has become a business for some, and you most likely have seen a proliferation of events, expos, and conferences, not to mention, hundreds upon hundreds of books on the subject. There are many fine organizations that are true not for profits and work for the greater good, and there are credible authors whose main goal is to help. However, there are others who exist purely to line their pockets with cash, and could not care less about your well- being.

We Have Seen It Time and Time Again

Those who believe in an afterlife do better in their grief recovery than those who don't. I am not suggesting that once we realize that our deceased loved ones still exist that we no longer grieve or experience periods of deep sadness. Of course we do. Despite our new found knowledge, the fact is that we no longer have them as part of our physical lives. What I am suggesting is that when you find yourself slipping into that deep chasm of despair, you do have a way of emerging. This is significant, as there are many who cannot make that statement. Those who have followed the steps outlined in this workbook are able to simply step back, review the astounding evidence that they have learned, review the personal proof that they have journaled, and move on with the knowledge that this physical existence is a mere blip in the continuum of life.

"I don't look at death in the same way others who never had after-death communication experiences do."
— TW, Denver Colorado

"It [the signs] proved to me that my son is still alive, just on another plane of existence –
just like he had always believed. They made me able to go on with my life because I was suicidal when
I thought my son just didn't exist anymore. These experiences saved my life, really."
— KR, Canterbury, Connecticut

The "formal" part of the video course in now completed.

Congratulations!

Additional videos, along with a recommended reading list, can be accessed via links at the bottom of the main video page (http://www.foreverfamilyfoundation.org/site/page/65). Although these videos are not considered to be essential, they are useful and interesting viewing for anybody who has followed the course so far. The recommended reading list is a small sample of books that many have found to be helpful.

If needed, use this area for extra writing space.   *Continued from page _____*

What You Need to Know Before, During and After a Session with a Medium

By Forever Family Foundation

❝ *This guide has been created to share the current knowledge and evolving information on mediumship in a way that will assist anyone considering sitting with a medium with hopes for a meaningful reading and positive experience. It is not meant to provide any therapeutic guidance nor does it suggest that by following the suggestions in this guide an evidential reading is guaranteed.*

"In order for humans to survive and evolve, we must come to accept the fact that we are spiritual beings having a physical experience. Moreover, in order for us to heal and transform, we must 1) develop the capacity to connect with a larger spiritual reality, 2) receive its wisdom and compassion, and 3) change our consciousness and behavior accordingly."

— *Dr. Gary E. Schwartz, Author*
The Afterlife Experiments

❝ *Life after death is not physical. Literally, it is nonsensical. The dead, having left the physical plane, cannot be experienced through the five senses which we normally associate with perception. Higher senses are needed to perceive them as what may be called energy, but the term should not be confused with its use in physics.*

Energy here means something like the emanation of being, something that can elicit a resonance within us. Some of us are "attuned," while many of us cannot quite quicken our inner resources to receive what comes to us. But all of us are addressed. All of us are called. We have but to learn and listen."

— *Dr. Jeffrey Kane*
Vice President for Academic Affairs
Long Island University

Q. What is a medium?

A medium is a person who claims to have the ability to communicate with non-physical entities. People often refer to these entities as the dead, spirit, or discarnates – all referring to persons no longer in the physical. Some mediums also claim to be able to communicate with "angels" or "spirit guides" who were never in the physical but whose purpose is to help and guide those who are.

Q. What is the purpose of a medium?

Although many may differ on the answer to this question, Forever Family Foundation believes that the sole purpose of a medium is to provide specific evidence that we survive our physical deaths. The evidence often proves to facilitate healing effects for those in grief, but it is the pure evidence that is given without conscious interpretation on the part of the medium that is important.

Q. A brief history of mediumship.

Mediumship is by no means a new phenomenon. Some would argue that many ancient philosophers as well as spiritual and religious figures gained insight from this practice. In the United States, the Fox Sisters are generally thought of as the impetus for the investigation of mediumship. The sisters provided much evidence by contacting entities that were thought to be responsible for strange sounds and activities in their Hydesville, New York home. An era of Spiritualism and Spiritism followed, incorporating religious practices with mediumship.

Q. Have mediums been studied by scientists?

Mediumship has been investigated since the early 1800s by some of the great minds of science, most of who came to the conclusion that the evidence of survival presented by mediums strongly suggested an afterlife. The list of these scientists and researchers from the past is extensive and includes members of the most prestigious scientific organizations from the fields of physics, chemistry and psychology. Some of the esteemed scientists from the past that have studied mediumship, deathbed visions, and apparitions include Pierre & Marie Curie, Dr. Alfred Russel Wallace, Dr. Charles Richet, Frederick W.H. Myers, Esq., Sir Oliver Lodge, Dr. James Hyslop, Sir Arthur Conan Doyle, Judge John Worth Edmonds, Sir William Crookes, Dr. Richard Hodgson, Dr. Robert Crookall, and many others. All came to the conclusion that something survives physical death. Modern day mediumship research continued in various universities, including the University of Virginia and the University of Arizona, and more recently at the Windbridge Institute for Applied Research in Human Potential under the direction of Dr. Julie Beischel.

Q. Are there different types of mediumship?

Mediumship is generally broken down into three category types:

• Mental Mediumship
This is the most prevalent form of mediumship today, and the type to which most people have been exposed. It refers to communication with spirit through forms of telepathy. It is thought that, since consciousness survives physical death, telepathy is not limited to those that are embodied. Although

the actual mechanism that enables this process has yet to be scientifically identified, mediums describe the ability to "raise their vibratory level" to facilitate communication with those in spirit form. According to mental mediums, spirit makes themselves known to them through the senses of seeing, hearing, feeling, smelling, tasting, and knowing.

• Trance Mediumship

Some believe that trance mediumship is actually a form of mental mediumship, and explain the process of spirit using the medium's mind to convey thought. Trance mediums remain conscious during the process, but describe allowing their conscious mind to recede into the background as they allow spirit to "take over." There is evidently a difference between "light trance" where the medium has awareness of the information coming through, and "deep trance" where the medium may not have recall of the process. Deep trance mediums were popular during the Victorian Era. In more recent times "channelers" have been witnessed going into a deep trance in which they become "occupied" by spirit entities who deliver messages of deep importance and understanding.

• Physical Mediumship

Physical mediumship involves manifestations of energy that result in observable physical phenomena. This can involve loud noises, voices, materializations, levitations, movement of objects, etc. Some believe that this process occurs by spirit's use of the medium's energy, or a substance called "ectoplasm" that exudes from the medium. Most believe that the energy of the sitters is also important and required for the process to work. Physical mediumship sessions often include spirit entities taking over the body of the medium as they deliver messages to those in attendance. Although there are still physical mediums in practice today, this type of mediumship was much more prevalent in the prior century.

Q. How do you know when you are ready to see a medium?

Opinion varies as to when the time is right to seek the services of a medium. Many believe that intense grief can inhibit the process of spirit communication, and therefore recommend that a certain amount of time pass before trying to contact a deceased loved one through a medium. Another school of thought, taken from channeled writings, is that the newly deceased may go through a period of adjustment or confusion. Being able to communicate with the physical may be a "skill" that takes some time and assistance for a spirit entity to master. On the other hand, there are many reports of visitations and communication from spirit immediately after their passing. The bottom line – we believe the time is right to see a medium when you feel that you are ready.

Q. Is there a difference between a psychic and a medium?

You may have heard it said that all mediums are psychic, but not all psychics are mediums. We believe this to be true. There appears to be a distinct difference between the ability to extract information from the living and communication with the dead. There are many well-qualified psychics who apparently can read minds, auras, and predict futures – but have never been able to communicate with deceased entities. The problem is that many such psychics advertise themselves as mediums, claiming that "all psychic information comes from spirit." Although this possibility cannot be entirely dismissed, we strongly suspect that phenomena such as telepathy, remote viewing, precognition, etc. are very likely inherent to our nature and have nothing to do with spirit communication.

Q. How to find a reputable medium.

The first thing to decide is what you want to get out of the reading. If you are grieving, you most likely want to hear from a deceased loved one and would not want to go to a psychic. If your only goal is to seek information that might help you learn about your future or gain insight into your everyday life, a psychic is probably the person you would choose to visit. Since mediums are also psychic, it should be clearly defined which type of reading you seek before sitting with a medium. Personal recommendations are always good, but bear in mind that mediumship is by no means an exact science. One person's visit to a medium might be highly evidential, but another person might report an unproductive experience with the same medium. There are many factors that are at work in the process – perhaps a "resonance" among the spirit entity, the medium and the sitter is required for strong communication. However, research shows that good mediums have a higher percentage of meaningful readings. If a medium maintains a website, it makes sense to visit and evaluate things such as rates charged, affiliations, and experience as a practicing medium. Also take note of the other services listed on the website to determine if mediumship is the practitioner's primary job – a medium needs extensive work and consistent practice to become and remain proficient in spirit communication. There are very few organizations that independently evaluate mediumship evidence, but such sources should be utilized when available. However, one should be wary of websites that maintain a listing of "recommended" mediums without describing the process by which the mediums were selected and evaluated. Sometimes these sources only list mediums who pay to appear on their list, without regard to their ability determined by independent and impartial evaluation. Forever Family Foundation conducts a science-based Medium Certification Program that incorporates such rigid controls, and only Certified Mediums are listed on our website. This listing is maintained as a resource for visitors to the website and there is no cost to the mediums.

Q. Are some mediums fraudulent?

Mediumship is not unlike any other profession – it is not immune to unscrupulous and deceptive practitioners who prey on others. Fraudulent mediums use such practices as "cold reading" where they look for body language clues and repeat general information. However, although such frauds do exist, it is more likely that you might chance upon a medium who is well intentioned, but lacks the necessary ability and experience to be consistent.

Q. Should you trust a medium who guarantees a connection?

Absolutely not! Every legitimate medium knows that the process is often subtle and subject to many factors not within their control. Although the better mediums make connections most of the time, even the best are occasionally unable to make any spirit contact for a particular sitter. There may be specific reasons that communication does not take place. For example, the sitter may be in grief and focused on hearing from one person in spirit, refusing to acknowledge other spirit entities. In addition, a loved one in spirit may not have the right conditions to facilitate communication with the physical world. Just as many people in the physical need the assistance of others to communicate with other realms of existence, those in spirit may also need their own guidance and help.

Q. Why do mediums charge for their services, and what should I expect to pay?

Although mediums engage in activities that are spiritual in nature, they must survive in the physical world just like the rest of us. They have families, mortgages, and all other fixed expenses that we all face. The fees charged by reputable mediums vary, and are usually flat rates for either a 30 minute or a 60 minute session. Although certain psychics advertise rates per minute, reputable mediums do not conduct their business in this fashion. If one should encounter a practitioner that claims to be a medium and wants to charge by the minute, you are probably dealing with a psychic and not a medium who regularly connects with spirit. The rates charged by mediums for a one hour reading are most commonly in the $100 to $400 range for an individual reading. (Higher prices are usually applicable when there is more than one person sitting before the medium.) Of course, factors such as geography, reputation, and proficiency of each individual medium influence the rates they charge. One should always determine the exact fee before deciding to schedule a reading.

Q. Is there any difference between a reading conducted in person versus over the telephone or via Skype?

Most people believe that an in-person reading results in a stronger connection among the medium, spirit, and the sitter. However, scientific research has found that in all manners of telepathic communication distance does not affect the process. In other words, whether a sitter is in the same room as the medium or 3,000 miles away, the information will be the same. In fact, most researchers prefer to conduct mediumship readings via the telephone, as it eliminates the possibility of the medium receiving clues from the sitter's body language. As such, the evidence received from a medium via the telephone might by interpreted to be more significant than if it had been received while face to face with the medium.

Q. What does it mean if your loved one does not come through in a reading?

It simply means that the conditions were not right. It should not be interpreted as an indication that the person in spirit does not love you or does not wish to communicate with you. The person in spirit may prefer to communicate with you directly, or is simply waiting for another time. It is also possible that the discarnate is busy with other worldly activities and not available at that particular time.

Q. Should you bring anything to the reading?

A recording device is strongly recommended. In our opinion, any medium who refuses to allow a session to be recorded should be avoided. There is often an abundance of information that is not recognized during the session, but later turns out to be significant. Some prefer to bring a pad and pencil. Any personal items should be well hidden, as it is in one's best interest to avoid giving obvious information to the medium. For example, a medium's statement that he/she has connected to your deceased son would hardly be evidential if you went to the reading wearing a necklace with a visible picture of him around your neck. Although some mediums find it helpful to hold an item that belonged to someone now in spirit, they should be able to make connections regularly without such aids. (See Psychometry in glossary)

Q. What to say and what NOT to say when making your appointment for a reading.

A medium needs only the basics when setting up an appointment – name and phone number should be sufficient. One should never divulge any personal information or give any indication of who they would like to contact.

Q. How should you prepare for the reading?

If you want evidence, make sure that you set the stage to gather evidence. Try to leave your expectations behind and simply remain open. Attempting to "will" contact with a specific entity may cause you to miss important evidence from others on the "other side" that may have messages for you. It is also thought that being focused on one specific entity may cause a block to receiving any information at all. Remember that the medium cannot command any particular spirit to make contact. Many believe that talking to your deceased loved ones, perhaps lighting a candle, or a silent prayer to the universe may enhance the experience.

Q. How to be a good sitter (person receiving the reading).

Reputable mediums do not want you to divulge information to them – it is their job to provide the evidence to you. However, it is important to the medium that you let them know whether or not a piece of information is correct. If the medium provides you with information that you deem to be correct, acknowledge this to the medium with simple phrases such as "I understand," or "that is true." On the other hand, if the information does not make any clear sense to you, a good response would be "I don't understand," or "that is not correct." Bear in mind that the experience can be very emotional, and sitters sometimes blurt out a tremendous amount of information to the medium. For example, if the medium tells you that he has your brother in spirit and he liked to play the guitar, don't respond by stating, "Yes, my brother Bill was an accomplished musician who once played with the Rolling Stones; he died in a motorcycle accident when he was 23, and he had a wife and son." (You get the picture!) Giving an abundance of information to the medium is not fair to the medium; it leaves little opportunity for the medium to provide specific and significant information, and can disturb the process. Also, if the medium is struggling, don't try to help out by making the information fit. Simply acknowledge that you don't understand and allow the medium go back to the person in spirit for more information. An accomplished medium understands that there will be pieces of information that do not appear to make sense – their job is only to convey what they receive and not evaluate the evidence.

Q. What is the difference between general and specific information during a reading?

Some information given by the medium might be true, but very general and might apply to a great many people. Other information is so specific that one cannot fathom how it could be reasonably guessed or inferred. For example, let's assume that you are 60 years old and sitting with a medium. The medium tells you that she has your grandmother in spirit who is communicating that she loves you, was a good cook, had trouble breathing before she died, enjoyed knitting, held the family together, and there is a Florida connection. All or most of this information would probably be true, and could apply to most grandmothers. However, if the same medium had your grandmother and told you her name was Julia, she died of pancreatic cancer, she knitted a blue and white sweater for you when you were five, she once called a family meeting and scolded your father, and she retired to Pensacola, Florida – that information, if true, would be considered to be significant and evidential. Some information, such as, "He loves you," or a question like, "Are you planning a move or job change?" cannot be verified and may not necessarily constitute evidence of communication with spirit. Especially significant information may sometimes take the form of facts you are not aware of during the reading, but are able to later investigate and find out to be true. In this type of an instance, it is significant in that it can be interpreted as refuting the notion that the medium was "reading your mind."

Q. If a medium is good, shouldn't he/she be able to give me my deceased loved one's name?

It is a common misconception that mediums should always be able to communicate the exact name of the deceased. The broad term of telepathy encompasses many elements that are not related to our five physical senses. Some mediums are very good at physical descriptions and personalities, but admittedly poor with receiving exact names. Think of it this way – if you are an entity of thought in the spirit world, and wish to communicate your name to the medium, how would you make this happen? If your name is George, perhaps you could project an image to the medium of George Washington, and hope that the medium interprets it correctly. Now suppose your name is Ilya – what image would you project? The discarnate might try to project a sound that will be heard by the medium, again hoping that the medium receives and interprets the sound correctly. This does happen frequently, which is why you hear many mediums repeating things like "….Joe…. Jay…. Jon." They may hear a one syllable name that begins with a "J" sound, but not the exact name.

It is important to evaluate the body of evidence given by a medium in its totality. If a medium provides 90% correct information, but does not get the name, this would still be considered strong evidence that communication with the deceased is taking place.

Q. What to do when the reading is over.

Listen to the tapes and consult your notes. For pieces of information that you don't understand, share this with family and friends who could possibly shed further light on this evidence. Also, in some cases, sitters report later hearing voices on the recording that were not heard during the reading (see Electronic Voice Phenomena in glossary) – be alert when listening. Some people report vivid dreams that include spirit "visits" soon after having a reading with a medium. Pay attention to such dreams and be sure to write them down as soon as you awake. It is recommended that you keep a pen, paper and small light near the bed for nighttime note taking. Many people that have extraordinary medium readings find it comforting to reflect back to the notes and recordings from the session at times, especially when they are feeling down. Evidence that a loved one survives can be extremely helpful in the grief process.

Q. Is it beneficial to return to the same medium?

The process of mediumship involves specific evidential information communicated from a discarnate entity which could not be reasonably guessed or inferred. Although qualified mediums most often do not recall the specifics of every reading they conduct, it is possible that some previous information that is stored in their subconscious might be repeated. Of course, a repeat visit to the same medium might reveal new evidence. If it is the pure evidence that the sitter seeks, however, it may be prudent to seek the services of a different qualified medium, especially if there is a short time frame between readings. If a particular medium is able to provide significant information when connecting to your loved one, the perceived need to visit the same medium is understandable. One might believe that their deceased loved one desires to communicate only through one particular medium. In addition, some may fear that by going to another medium, they open themselves for possible disappointment, as there is never a guarantee that a specific connection can be made. However, if your loved one is able to communicate through a particular medium, that does not mean this is the only channel available.

Q. Am I supposed to become a medium?

We all possess the ability to communicate "non-locally" with senses that often remain unused. The fact is that people receive after death communication all the time in many different ways. Mediums have honed these skills to the point where they can communicate with spirit entities on a consistent basis and have learned to present the evidence from spirit in a manner that is easily understood. They are also well-guided by spirit on how to deliver this information to those in grief. Some people, especially after suffering the loss of a loved one, interpret some after death communication received as a sign that they themselves were meant to be a medium. Furthermore, some people who go to a sitting with a medium are told by the medium (or spirit) that they have intuitive abilities of their own. While this statement may be true, many times a sitter will interpret this message as an indication that they must develop their own mediumship skills. Before embarking on such a path, people are encouraged to conduct serious self-exploration to determine if this is truly a career that they are meant to pursue, or a reaction in seeking meaning in the death of a loved one.

Q. Mediums and the media.

There have been quite a number of television shows in recent years that feature mediums. Although the evidence of spirit communication that is depicted appears to be extraordinary, one must realize the nature of television programming. Due to extensive editing, it can appear to some that certain mediums never convey incorrect information. This can give some people the wrong impression about the process of mediumship. Evidential mediums convey significant information the majority of the time. However, it is wrong to assume that any medium can be 100% accurate all of the time. Those who are unfamiliar with mediumship are cautioned to recognize this fact and have reasonable expectations about the process.

Q. What does it all mean?

A specific and evidential medium reading can have a profound effect on someone grieving the loss of a loved one. Let's face it – believing that a loved one still survives their physical death is perhaps the most effective form of therapy. On the other hand, an unsuccessful reading should not cause one to dismiss the possibility of an afterlife, nor should one question why a loved one would not want to make contact. Science has yet to determine the necessary components to successful communication. There may be many factors in play, including some sort of entanglement among the spirit, medium, and sitter. Mediumship is but one way of receiving communication – your contact may occur directly. Forever Family Foundation believes that we all have the capability of learning ways to directly continue a relationship with our deceased loved ones. Mediums provide a wonderful conduit to those in spirit, but personal experience can be life-changing. Although there has never been a formal study, it is clear that some individuals become addicted to mediums in desperate attempts to stay connected to deceased loved ones. For these people there is never enough evidence. We believe that it is healthy to seek evidence, but such confirmation should come from a variety of techniques and inner reflection. Sooner or later, the goal would be for the bereaved person to accept the totality of the evidence and resume the navigation of their physical life with purpose and meaning, as well as the acquired knowledge that relationships do not end with physical death.

Glossary of Terms

CHANNELERS – People who are able to go into trance and let a spirit entity take over their body, usually to provide spiritual wisdom and important information.

DISCARNATE – Describing an entity that no longer has a physical body.

ENTANGLEMENT – A term used in quantum theory to describe the way that particles of energy/matter can become correlated to predictably interact with each other.

ELECTRONIC VOICE PHENOMENA – Recordings of voice or voice-like sounds that are not audible to the human ear at the time of the recording, and is heard only during playback. The frequencies of these sounds are reportedly well below the range of sounds that can be perceived by the human ear.

NON-LOCAL COMMUNICATION – Communication that occurs without the assistance of any apparent mechanical or physical means, usually disregarding time and space.

PRECOGNITION – Acquiring information about future events through non-physical means.

PSYCHOMETRY – The supposed ability to discover facts about an event or person by touching inanimate objects associated with them.

REMOTE VIEWING – The process of gathering information from a distant target that is "unseen" to the viewer. This information is received by use of the viewer's mind or consciousness, and not via the known physical senses.

SITTER – The person receiving the reading from a medium.

SPIRIT – Referring to those entities who do not reside in the physical realm.

SPIRIT GUIDE – An entity not in the physical who is thought to offer help and guidance to those in the physical realm. Such guides refer to both those who once were incarnate and those who have always resided in higher realms of existence.

TELEPATHY – The transfer of thoughts, feelings and information through means other than the generally recognized physical senses.

MAKE A PLEDGE
CHANGE WORLD VIEW

Please consider a tax deductible donation to our
100% volunteer not-for-profit

Forever Family Foundation
222 Atlantic Avenue
Oceanside, New York 11572-2009

foreverfamilyfoundation.org

If needed, use this area for extra writing space. *Continued from page _____*